SUPER SPELLERS

SUPER SPELLERS

SEVEN STEPS
to
TRANSFORMING
Your
SPELLING
INSTRUCTION

MARK WEAKLAND

FOREWORD BY RICHARD GENTRY

Stenhouse
PUBLISHERS

www.stenhouse.com

Library of Congress Cataloging-in-Publication Data

Names: Weakland, Mark, author.
Title: Super spellers : seven steps to transforming your spelling instruction / Mark Weakland.
Description: Portland, Maine : Stenhouse Publishers, [2017] | Includes bibliographical references.
Identifiers: LCCN 2017016464 (print) | LCCN 2017039944 (ebook) | ISBN 9781625311030 (ebook) | ISBN 9781625311023 (pbk. : alk. paper)
Subjects: LCSH: English language--Orthography and spelling--Study and teaching. | English language--Composition and exercises--Study and teaching. | Reading.
Classification: LCC LB1574 (ebook) | LCC LB1574 .W37 2017 (print) | DDC 372.63/2--dc23
LC record available at https://lccn.loc.gov/2017016464

Cover design, interior design, and typesetting by Lucian Burg, LU Design Studios, Portland, ME

Manufactured in the United States of America

PRINTED ON 30% PCW
RECYCLED PAPER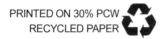

23 22 21 20 19 18 17   9 8 7 6 5 4 3 2 1

To dedicated and caring teachers everywhere

Contents

Foreword

Mark Weakland fully grasps an aspect of spelling instruction that is unknown to some literacy educators: *Spelling knowledge is essential for reading achievement.* In *Super Spellers,* he gives you best-practice spelling strategies that will transform your literacy classroom.

Mark writes for all teachers—those who already have a spelling curriculum in place as well as those who are just getting started. As you read this book, you will appreciate Mark's gift of getting to the crux of complex ideas and explaining them cogently and unerringly in ways we can all understand. Here, in his own words, Mark states what we all need to know:

> *Brain and cognition research support, in a big way, the idea that effective spelling instruction not only activates reading circuitry but also creates the neural pathways and cognitive "wiring" that lead to higher reading achievement. Over the last ten years, studies have shown, with ever increasing degrees of specificity, that the spelling-reading connection is real, and that it consists of multiple processing systems in the brain that coordinate actions to enable reading.*

In this book, Mark shows you exactly how to bring the effective spelling instruction you need to your literacy teaching. His message is believable because he offers his firsthand experience with poor spellers who were poor readers, and then shares his personal journey to better practice. By immersing himself deeply in the latest research in cognitive psychology and neuroscience and bringing to bear his own deep, wide, and thoughtful experience as a literacy teacher, Mark connects the dots from the latest research to exemplary best practice for teaching spelling, reading, and writing.

What I like most about *Super Spellers,* beyond its appeal as a treasure trove of purposeful and essential best teaching practice, is Mark's ability to take deep ideas, boil them down, and cook up a broth for healing some of our most egregious literacy ills of the past while at the same time nourishing our growth as teachers of spelling—and thereby of reading and writing. The benefits Mark serves up in

Super Spellers are numerous, extensive, and—for many—unexpected. Decades of pushing spelling instruction to the back burner can now be corrected.

Mark is a wordsmith. He presents deep ideas and best practice brilliantly, with boundless readability, connected to relatable classroom examples and experiences. Not only will you learn a lot, but you will also enjoy reading this book.

So, now you are ready to join Mark on an incredible journey. Pause one moment to ponder this important message from Mark:

> *All of this is tremendously exciting. By emphasizing best-practice spelling instruction, we stand ready not only to accelerate the achievement of our typical students but also to help students with dyslexia and other reading difficulties begin to build better functioning neural pathways, thereby making reading easier for them, both now and later in life.*

Super Spellers is the kind of staff development book that surfaces only a few times in a decade—a book that brilliantly, concisely, and concretely connects the latest research to best practice. It's an enjoyable read that will give you immediate ideas to take back to your classroom. You know how you have a few books you come back to over and over? This is one of those. I predict that this book will be an important contribution to reading education today and for decades to come.

J. Richard Gentry, PhD

Source: Weakland, Mark. 2016. "Spelling Is at the Heart of the Reading Process." February 13. http://www.markweaklandliteracy.com/blog/spelling-is-at-the-heart-of-the-reading-process.

Acknowledgments

I wish to thank everyone at Stenhouse Publishing; Dr. Richard Gentry, whose work has informed my own teaching and whose insightful critique of my proposal provided a touchstone for the writing of this book; Kathy Snyder, who taught me a lot about literacy coaching and helped me improve my assessments; the elementary school teachers and students of Ferndale, Turkeyfoot Valley, and Armstrong school districts; and Dawn Walters, Cristina Bowman, Jill Tedesco, Kathy O'Donnell, Tara Yeterian, Hope Davidson, and Alysha Gallagher, who went out of their way to help me with spelling activities, and classroom pictures. Special thanks to Tori Bachman, whose wise guidance and encouragement empowered me to turn ideas into reality.

Introduction

Are you a confident and accurate speller? Do you spell every word correctly when you write a birthday note or compose a letter home to parents? Do you write in ink because you have no anxiety about misspelled words? Or are you like me, an anxious speller who prints in pencil and gives thanks for his spell-check program every time he sits down at the computer?

As a kid, I aced my weekly elementary school spelling tests. But the writing I did in stories and book reports was always peppered with spelling mistakes. Although I no longer write book reports, spelling is still a problem for me. Occasionally, my lack of ability causes me embarrassment. Once, at a teachers' professional development workshop, I was part of a group that was told to make a poster on intervention programs. The group elected me to be their scribe. I have "writing-in-public-ophobia" so I have no idea how I allowed this to happen, but nonetheless, there I was, Sharpie in hand and posterboard in front of me. At one point I carefully printed "excellerate progress." When a team member politely asked if I had meant to spell the word *accelerate*, I tried to cover my embarrassment with a bit of wit. "No," I replied, "I meant *excellerate*. It means picking up the pace in a most excellent way."

Unlike my wife, who, like most accomplished spellers, simply knows what words look like, I can't seem to easily see words in my head, and when I write them down, I don't know if they "look right" or not. *Rhythmical* never looks correct to me, and I'm just as likely to write *hesitent* as *hesitant*. As for *silhouette*, forget it. Spell checker, here I come.

Through my midtwenties, I never thought much about my spelling weakness. And I certainly never thought about how others spell. But that changed when, at age twenty-seven, I became a teacher. In my first year, I began to wonder why some children made a perfect score on their spelling test every week but misspelled many words on their authentic writing. Later, I began to wonder if my spelling instruction was ultimately helping or hurting my students' achievement. The children in my special education classroom came to me at least a year behind in reading and writing, and many of them didn't like to read and write. If these students were going to reach critical grade-level benchmarks and develop the ability to enjoy reading a book and writing a story, then every aspect of my instruction, from spelling and phonics to grammar and vocabulary, needed to go toward boosting their reading and writing skills. If my spelling instruction wasn't doing anything to steadily improve students' ability to read and write, or, heaven forbid, if my instruction was holding them back, then why bother to do it at all?

To set the stage for this book, I'm going to jump back in time for a moment. Travel with me to the year 1991, when the United States was joining a coalition of countries to push Saddam Hussein out of Kuwait, Kentucky Fried Chicken was changing its name to KFC, and I was a first-year teacher with a ponytail running a self-contained learning support classroom for fourth and fifth graders.

Like many teachers, I can clearly remember all the children I taught in my first year of teaching. What a crew! Each of my sixteen students was identified as having a specific learning disability or an emotional disturbance. Some of my kids did quite well on their weekly twenty-word spelling tests. I remember Randy and Jessica in particular. Week after week, on Friday afternoons when I handed back the tests, those two would grin like Cheshire cats. Another A+! But for all their spelling "ability," Randy and Jessica were unable to read beyond a first-grade level, and they rarely spelled words accurately while writing. This perplexed me. How could they do so well on their spelling tests yet struggle so much with their reading and writing?

Meanwhile, other students consistently bombed their weekly spelling tests. Jaclyn comes to mind. She was a kindhearted child and a worker bee who always concentrated and completed assignments, even when my classroom was chaotic. Jaclyn's parents were supportive and helped her practice her spelling at home. Yet week after week, Jaclyn failed to spell more than thirteen or fourteen words correctly on her twenty-word list. She made random and seemingly careless mistakes, slipping in an extra vowel, failing to use the digraph –ck for the k sound in black, or spelling in a nonsensical way (creature spelled craechr). I saw the disappointment in Jaclyn's eyes each time I handed back her spelling tests, and it broke my heart. This child was studying, practicing with her parents, and working hard in school. Why was she doing so poorly on her spelling tests?

By the end of my second year, I knew I couldn't in good conscience allow some children to suffer the humiliation of consistently awful scores. I also realized that the basal spelling program, which sucked up a fair amount of my time, did little to improve student achievement in either reading or writing. So I began to create my own program, using Nina Traub's book *Recipe for Reading* as the foundation. I taught fewer sounds and patterns every week, I made sure I used the same weekly patterns to teach spelling and phonics, and I got better at showing the kids how the two were connected. I also began to teach to mastery, repeating the spelling patterns for a second or third week if students hadn't fully learned them. By the end of my first six years of classroom teaching, I still didn't know much about how spelling developed, or how reading, writing, and spelling were connected, but I was regularly offering two and sometimes three spelling lists to my students, reteaching lessons when I thought I needed to, and using a writing-workshop approach that emphasized spelling while writing.

What did I learn from teaching spelling to students with individualized education plans? I learned that they experienced more spelling success when their lessons focused on fewer sounds and patterns, when their lists were differentiated, and when their instruction didn't proceed at a one-size-fits-all pace. I also learned that teaching children to pay attention to spelling in writing, and giving them strategies to first find and then fix their spelling mistakes, made them more independent in their writing and lowered their number of misspellings. But I still had much more to learn.

Fast forward to 2010. After working as an educational consultant for a number of years, I went back to teaching. My assignment as a Title I reading specialist was to coteach in third-, fifth-, and sixth-grade classrooms, run pull-out intervention groups, and sit on data analysis teams. Whenever I sat and looked at reading scores, I was intrigued by the patterns I saw. Roughly 90 to 95 percent of our school's kindergarten children were reaching the Developmental Reading Assessment and DIBELS benchmarks by the end of the year. A smaller percentage of first graders made the benchmarks. This decline continued through second grade. By October of any given year, 55 to 70 percent of all third graders were at benchmark level. Many of the lowest-achieving third graders ended up in my cotaught "corrective reading" classroom. Of these children, at least half were reading on a first-grade level, many struggled with the basal program's third-grade spelling lists, and most produced authentic writing that showed confusion about basic sounds, patterns, and conventions. Thus, I saw *gam* for *game, techr* for *teacher*, and *iceing* for *icing*.

During my first year back in the classroom, my cooperating teacher and I closely followed the basal reading curriculum. We read the anthology stories out loud, played the stories on the CD, assigned workbook and practice book pages, gave writing prompts from the teacher's manual, and followed the basal's scope and sequence of weekly spelling words. By the end of the year, the majority of our students had grown by a half-year or less, which was the same growth pattern that the first- and second-grade corrective reading classrooms experienced.

The following year, we broke free of our basal series and created an alternative program that, among other things, taught spelling and phonics using syllable types, used more direct and explicit instruction during spelling lessons, used word study activities, and emphasized spelling in writing. Lo and behold, our students showed strong gains in their reading scores! For three years in a row, 80 to 90 percent of the children in our classroom made *at least* a year's worth of growth on their reading benchmark scores. Some grew by as much as a year and a half and even two years. Another third-grade teacher, one who knew a great deal about reading and writing, decided to deviate from the basal, too. By the end of the year, the children in her "low average" group were also making strong gains. Meanwhile, the scores from the corrective reading groups in first and second grade, which had made fewer changes to their spelling, reading, or writing instruction, continued to experience lower growth rates.

What I took away from these classroom experiences was the passion to want to do something about traditional but ineffective approaches to reading, writing, and spelling instruction. I am convinced that when you trade traditional spelling instruction for an approach that is developmental, mastery based, and closely tied to reading and writing, you greatly increase the chances that your students will become not only better spellers, but also better readers and writers.

Spelling is not the only key to reading and writing success, but it is an important one. Why? During spelling instruction, you build your students' ability to recognize words. Word recognition, in turn, leads to reading and writing fluency. When reading and writing fluency improve to automaticity, students have a greater capacity to concentrate on and be successful with reading comprehension and written expression. In other words, when children effortlessly and automatically decode words while reading or encode words while writing, they are able to devote their full attention to making meaning. All of this leads to deeper comprehension and more thorough written expression.

The type of spelling instruction you engage in can make a world of difference to students, especially for children who struggle to read and write. So let's do something about spelling! I spent the bulk of my classroom-teaching career working with low-achieving students, and I saw them fail when my instruction was ineffective and flourish when my instruction was based on best practice. Because I know that excellent teaching is the number-one school-based factor in creating student success, I am especially excited about helping teachers transform any spelling instruction that relies on worksheets, inflexible content sequences, and less-than-effective instructional techniques.

How to Use This Book

The first goal of this book is to give you, the teacher, information that you can reflect upon and then apply in your classroom. But this book's ultimate goal is to enable children in elementary schools to become better spellers, and thereby better readers and writers, through a process that has less to do with the acquisition of facts and more to do with the acquisition of knowledge.

If you feel stuck within the confines of an ineffective spelling sequence from a basal (core-reading) program, this book provides a transformative path, one that will move you from weekly "memorize-and-move-on" word lists and teacher-directed "one-size-fits-all" instruction to a differentiated and developmental instructional approach that gives students the tools they need to become metacognitive, strategic spellers.

If you are teaching in a balanced literacy or reading and writing workshop classroom but still see some students struggle with spelling, then this book will give you a fresh look at the developmental aspects of spelling. Even more, it will give you new ideas on spelling assessment, explicit and direct instruction, and word-study strategies and activities that can be easily woven into the reading and writing that's already happening in your classroom.

Finally, if your school uses a stand-alone spelling program, such as *Words Their Way* or *Spelling Connections*, this book will give ways to address some of the things you know aren't working in your current program. It will also provide new and different ideas for organizing and presenting words and using activities that bolster instruction and lead to greater student learning.

Research has revealed (and continues to point to) ways to teach spelling that are more effective than those offered in many traditional programs. The most effective spelling instruction is

- **direct and explicit** (Levin and Aram 2013; Rosenshine 2012),
- **systematic and sequential** (Gentry and Graham 2010),
- **focused** (Rosenshine 2012),
- **differentiated** (Invernizzi and Hayes 2004; Morris et al. 1995a),

- **strategy based** (Adams 2011),
- **mastery based** (Dewitz and Jones 2013; Invernizzi and Hayes 2004),
- **centered on sound, pattern, and meaning** (McCandliss, Wise, and Yoncheva 2015; Moats 2005/2006; Perfetti 1997; Graham 1998),
- **based on the theory that spelling is developmental** (Henderson 1990; Treiman and Bourassa 2000; Levin and Aram 2013), and
- **intimately linked to reading and writing** (Adams 2011; Gentry and Graham 2010; McCandliss, Wise, and Yoncheva 2015; Reed 2012).

In *Super Spellers*, you will have the opportunity to look at each of these concepts, as well as consider materials, types of instruction, and assessments that speak to them all.

A Note to Teachers Using Basal (Core-Reading) Programs

The section above lists the components that make for the most effective spelling instruction. To be clear, basal spelling programs contain many of these elements. They are often systematic and explicit. They are rooted in the conventions of English spelling. They have plans for teaching strategies and activities. And they have ties to reading and writing.

However, basal spelling programs lack vigor, depth, and flexibility. They may not be systematic enough. The scope of what they cover is often too big, which means they introduce too many sound spellings, patterns, or conventions in their lessons. Their instructional sequences go by too quickly and may not be in an order that makes sense, especially when compared with your sequence of grammar and reading skills. Sometimes the sequences and the scope of what they cover duplicate what is covered in grammar lessons (and vice versa). And many traditional spelling programs are not based on the philosophy of mastery learning.

There are other problems. Basal-based spelling programs may lack explicit links to reading and writing. Also, these programs present "everything under the sun" but fail to explicitly point out what concepts and activities are most important. When the expectation is that everything presented in the manual will be taught and completed (because your district expects fidelity to the basal program), then instruction is diluted and academic gains may be diminished. More becomes less. Additionally, the teacher's manuals of basal spelling programs may fail to emphasize or even mention easy-to-implement and highly effective instructional practices, such as the consistent use of direct and explicit instruction or having kindergarten and first-grade children look at and then say the teacher-provided correct spelling of their invented spelling (Levin and Aram 2013). Finally, traditional programs may underemphasize student self-monitoring and the utilization of spelling strategies, as well as the adoption of a developmental stance in which strategies are taught to children if and when they need them.

Super Spellers begins to rectify these failings, and it does so without asking you to eliminate your basal program, ditch your scope and sequence, or insert an entirely new program into your already very busy day. But if you are stuck with an ineffective basal-based spelling program, this book gives you a way to transform your program into instruction that explicitly ties together encoding, decoding, reading, and writing. This process won't take place overnight. Rome wasn't built in a day, right? But with a bit of determination, you can make it happen, over many months and even a few years, step by step by step.

Seven Steps to Super Spelling

In literature and lore, seven is a magic number. There are seven dwarfs, seven seals, seven deadly sins, Seven Wonders of the World, and so on. Although some might claim it takes magic to help our kids become better spellers, readers, and writers, I've found that it really just takes a bit of time and effort. But the results may seem magical! Thus, I present the overview of how to transform spelling instruction as seven "magical" steps:

1. **Understand Theory and Practice.** The first step asks us to understand that spelling is developmental, that specific types of instruction lead to greater amounts of growth, and that teaching children how to spell includes teaching them to be strategy users. We must also understand that sounds, patterns, and meanings lie at the heart of spelling instruction, that poor spelling and poor reading are connected, and that because spelling is at the heart of the reading process, the most effective spelling instruction teaches children to read.

2. **Assess Spelling Knowledge.** Assessing spelling knowledge starts at the beginning of the year with spelling inventories, writing sample analyses, and reading assessments. It continues through the year with weekly spelling quizzes and tests, notes on word study activities, and the regular examination of writing samples. Assessment is essential for understanding where students are developmentally as well as for differentiating instruction. When instruction and assessment work together, such as during test-study-test cycles, retrieval practice, and instant error correction, greater learning occurs.

3. **Focus Scope and Sequence.** A focused scope and sequence helps students achieve spelling and reading mastery. To focus, slow the rate of movement through your spelling sequence, narrow the scope of what you teach, and reteach information as necessary, especially for students in the early stages of spelling development who must master the essential skill of matching letters to sounds. Focus also means creating word lists that support instruction by taking previously published lists and modifying them to create new ones.

4. **Bring More Words.** To create more effective instruction, bring many words to your lessons. These words are built from the sounds, patterns, affixes, roots, or conventions that you picked for your refocused lessons and spelling lists. Bringing in more words enables you to teach a wider variety of word-study activities, use a wider variety of assessment techniques, and more easily differentiate for two or three groups of students.

5. **Teach Strategies.** Spelling strategies are crucial if children are to learn how to spell rather than what to spell. Thus, teach children how to self-monitor and be metacognitive, as well as how to use strategies while writing, reading, and taking a test. The strategies you teach can include using sounds and letters, using mnemonics, using meaning, using visualizing, and using patterns (analogy), including the seven syllable types.

6. **Teach Activities.** Teach spelling through activities that show how sound, pattern, and meaning are at the heart of spelling, as well as activities that can incorporate a variety of developmental stages, from sound-letter matching to etymology and morphology.

7. **Build Opportunities.** Finally, build opportunities to connect spelling to reading, from presenting decodable sentences to giving students the chance to read in as many places and in as many ways as possible. Also, build opportunities to connect spelling to writing, especially in authentic writing situations, from journal writing to digital platforms, such as writing apps and online blogs.

This is a lot to consider, I know. But we'll take it one step at a time. The transformation from so-so to super doesn't happen in an instant, like mild-mannered Clark Kent dashing into the nearest phone booth to emerge seconds later as Superman. Rather, think of it more like Clark Kent and a couple of friends purposefully strolling into the nearest library and sitting down for a few hours to learn, think, and expand upon their already impressive powers.

CHAPTER 1

Understand Theory and Practice

IN THIS CHAPTER

- We will discuss why spelling instruction is tremendously important. Spelling lies at the heart of the reading process. When children learn how to spell, when they practice encoding in specific ways, and when their attention is drawn to the sounds, patterns, and meanings in words and syllables, they become fluent readers more quickly.

- We will also examine what best-practice spelling instruction consists of (and what it doesn't consist of).

- Finally, we will learn that spelling is developmental, a process that occurs in stages over time. The development of spelling ability is different for different children, necessitating differentiation within our lessons and units of study.

Learning occurs in leaps and bounds, steps and strides, fits and starts. My greatest leap in learning about spelling and its role in literacy occurred when I left my job as an education consultant and went back to teaching children. I was able to compare the "book learning" I had gained during my consulting with what actually happens with children as they learn to read and write.

While working in kindergarten classrooms, I witnessed children taking the sounds of language and turning them into the letter symbols of written English (Figure 1.1), and I saw them acquiring reading, writing, and spelling skills at different rates. By the time kindergarten ended, some children were reading on an end-of-first-grade level and writing entire paragraphs with many correctly used spelling patterns, whereas others were just squeaking by the end-of-the-year reading benchmarks and writing simple sentences using words that showed basic sound-letter correspondence.

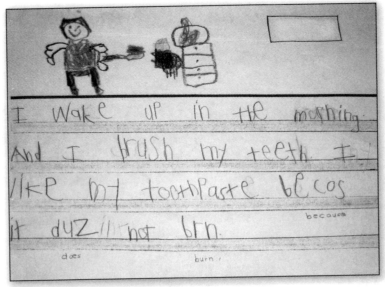

Figure 1.1 Kindergarten sound-letter correspondence

Simultaneously, while teaching in a corrective reading class, I saw older students who were confused about how to spell vowel sounds, even though they had received spelling instruction on vowels in first and second grades. As I worked with these students, I began to understand how typical methods of spelling instruction (fast-paced sequence, broad scope, worksheets, lack of discussion about how words work, and so on) failed to make permanent some important elements of spelling, writing, and reading (Figure 1.2).

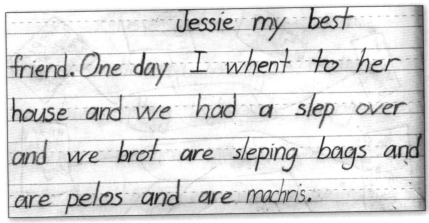

Figure 1.2 Third-grade writing showing spelling confusion

My journey to understanding spelling and its place in literacy has taken more than twenty years, and I have yet to arrive at a final destination. But I understand much more about spelling instruction than when I first started teaching, and I am thankful for the many hardworking and brilliant researchers, writers, and teachers from whom I have learned. By sharing what took me decades to understand, I hope I can help you shave years off the process of transforming your spelling instruction. Let's start by trying to truly understand spelling and its relationship to reading and writing.

Spelling Is at the Heart of the Reading Process

During my years of teaching, I saw firsthand that poor spellers were poor readers. Fortunately, I also saw how certain types of spelling instruction helped children become better readers. But I never really connected the spelling and reading dots in a big way. Now, however, after digesting research studies that explore the connections among cognition, brain structure, and literacy, and after reading what writers and researchers such as Richard Gentry, Louisa Moats, and Dan Willingham have to say about the importance of spelling for reading, I know that spelling is foundational to reading.

Brain and cognition research supports the idea that effective spelling instruction not only activates reading circuitry but also creates the neural pathways and cognitive "wiring" that lead to higher reading achievement. Over the last ten years, studies have shown that the spelling-reading connection is real, and that it consists of multiple processing systems in the brain that coordinate actions to enable reading (Adams 2011; Dehaene and Cohen 2011; Rapp and Lipka 2011; Norton, Kovelman, and Petitto 2007).

Aided by functional magnetic resonance imaging technology that allows researchers to see the brain working in real time and by an increasingly sophisticated understanding of how reading develops, researchers now know that reading is a complex interaction between a number of brain "processors": phonological, orthographic, sound-symbol, and context and meaning. In a student's early years (i.e., elementary school, especially the primary grades), there exists in the brain a greater emphasis on phonological and sound-symbol processing. Later, the orthographic area gains importance, eventually storing thousands of words in entirety, readying them for later use in reading and spelling.

Creating mental images of correctly spelled words is an act that never ceases. Even as adults, we add words to our brain-based repository of spelling representations. Just this year, after writing and revising a series of science articles, I added *camouflage* to my repository. *Camouflage* was a word I could never seem to spell correctly. But after reading it and spelling it literally dozens of times, the word is now permanently etched into my gray matter.

It may be helpful to think of the repository of word spellings as a "dictionary in your brain" (Gentry 2015; Willingham 2015). Because our brains activate this dictionary and draw upon it during fluent reading, it is critical that we help children develop their own dictionaries, for well-developed dictionaries can lead to higher fluency and deeper comprehension.

As I understand it, effective spelling instruction activates the brain circuitry that stores, in the orthographic processing area, the following: letter pairs (such as *ph*, *sh*, and *ch*), graphemes and morphemes (patterns, such as *ame*, *ight*, and *unk*, as well as affixes and roots), and complete words (such as *chunk*, *shameful*, and *orthographic*). This storing mirrors a child's reading, writing, and spelling development: first words are built up from separate stored sound-letter matches, then chunks, and later whole words. From eye-motion studies and cognition studies, we know that fluent reading is dependent upon the lightning-fast and effortless recognition of *entire words*. Thus, one of our teaching goals should be to help students store thousands of word spellings in their brains.

This storing is a critical component of the reading process, a process that combines the fluent and effortless matching of words a reader sees with word meanings and word spellings. The process is analogous to a walk down a forest path. As you enter the woods, your brain, stocked with literally thousands of concepts, stands ready to match the concepts with whatever you see. As you look around, your constantly thinking brain automatically and accurately matches each seen thing with a concept. That fluffy green stuff? Moss. The jumping gray thing? Squirrel! Each visual image is automatically matched with a name (or names) and a meaning (or meanings). You see and recognize a hemlock, some ferns, a hickory tree, a stream or a bubbling brook, a black-capped chickadee, a woodpecker (is it a downy or a hairy?), a rock with lichen on it, and so on. Of course, the process is more than simple "image calling," just as reading is more than "word calling." As you walk, you also make meaning in a much larger way, and you may notice thoughts arising, such as *I wonder if that woodpecker is finding food for its young*, and *Wow, this is a spectacular spring day!*

This act of cognition is similar to how the reading brain works. Scientists have shown that upon seeing a word (essentially a set of squiggles) on a page or screen, the brain's reading circuitry coordinates various storage and processing areas in roughly a quarter of a second or less. All this storage, processing, and coordination ensure that when a reader looks at a word, the reader knows the sound of the word, the meaning of the word, and the conventional spelling of the word. In the end, brain action enables a fluent reader to read this sentence—*The tired man fill asleep on the bead*—identify any errors, and quickly swap in the correct words for the incorrect.

When, through effective spelling instruction, children encounter dozens of spelling patterns and hundreds (if not thousands) of words, their brain dictionaries expand and deepen. Put another way, over months and years of practice, children develop word permanency. Willingham specifically puts it in terms of spelling, saying that children "develop an increasing number of mental representations that allow them to identify words by their appearance, i.e., by their spelling" (Willingham 2014).

One fascinating literacy and cognition study, authored in 2015 by Bruce McCandliss and his colleagues at Stanford University, seems to give strong support to the following important points:

- Reading instruction that emphasizes decoding (phonics) and encoding (spelling) is more effective than instruction that doesn't.

- The way in which words and word parts are taught affects how efficiently brains call up words a day later and learn new words.

- Certain methods of direct and explicit instruction in the areas of letter-sound correspondences and spelling patterns (phonics) increase the likelihood that readers will develop efficient decoding skills.

- And most amazingly, certain methods of instruction actually promote the left-lateralization of the brain, strengthening the left-hemisphere brain circuits that are most needed for the decoding of sub-lexical units. In other words, specific types of instruction set up positive feedback loops for reading word chunks, allowing poor readers to simultaneously activate *and* build brain circuitry that is both underused in their current state of reading development and critical for future fluent reading.

All of this is tremendously exciting. By emphasizing best-practice spelling instruction, you stand ready to not only accelerate the achievement of your typical students, but also help students with dyslexia and other reading difficulties begin to build better-functioning neural pathways, thereby making reading easier for them, both now and later in life.

Spelling Instruction: Alone and Together

Teaching spelling well is something of an instructional paradox. Spelling should be taught as a stand-alone subject (Gentry and Graham 2010). During this stand-alone time, word study occurs, patterns are explored, strategies are explained and practiced, and spelling activities take place. All this activity leads children to the mastery and control of word parts, as well as the understanding of how sound, pattern, and meaning come together to produce correctly spelled words.

Yet spelling should *also* be directly and explicitly linked to reading (including vocabulary) and writing (including grammar). It is a good idea to tell your students that spelling and reading are two sides of the same coin (Ehri 2000) and show them that encoding (spelling) is the flip side of decoding (reading).

Spelling is a skill that enables fluent writing and reading. In turn, more reading and writing enables more fluent spelling. Reading widely exposes kids to more words and provides better background knowledge of how commonly used words are spelled. Writing widely does the same thing. When children write, they see words as they spell them, they see words as they revise and read their writing again, and they see words as they read their writing one last time, sharing it with a buddy, small group, or larger audience.

We cannot, however, rely on writing and reading to teach students new spellings and new spelling skills. Although reading and writing do lead to spelling gains, the gains are not large (Graham and Harris 2016). Teaching spelling directly leads to greater gains in spelling competence. But stand-alone spelling instruction is not enough if we want our students to become proficient writers with mature writing skills. When we look at the big picture, the best way to promote spelling development is to teach a combination of the two approaches (Graham and Harris 2016).

Spelling Ability Doesn't Develop from Memorizing a Weekly Word List

The most effective spelling instruction is *not* a weekly routine in which you give your students a list of loosely connected words, have them complete worksheets and write the words numerous times at home, give them a test at the end of the week where they regurgitate the words from memory, and then move on to another list of loosely connected words. This "memorize-and-move-on" routine does little to help children become better spellers, readers, and writers. In my opinion, children who become accomplished spellers in classrooms that use a "memorize-and-move-on" program learn to spell *in spite of* the program.

This is not to say that memory does not play a part in spelling. It does. Earlier, we learned that spelling is at the heart of the reading process, and that a well-developed "dictionary" of words in the brain is a component that is critical to fluent reading. This dictionary is built through well-designed word study, strategy use, and a great deal of practice in reading, writing, and spelling. In the end, letter-sound relationships, spelling patterns, and eventually entire words are committed to memory.

In addition, spelling involves committing to memory the specific letter sequences of a few irregular words, such as *of, said,* and *was.* These letter sequences must be practiced until the whole words enter the orthographic repository. Spelling also involves the remembering of conventions (such as syllable types or ways of spelling plurals) and strategies (such as spelling a word by thinking about its meaning). Once committed to memory, word conventions and spelling strategies can be accessed and used to spell unknown words.

Spelling instruction that is mastery based, strategy based, differentiated, and centered on sound, pattern and meaning is something very different from instruction that consists of little more than introducing and then testing on a memorize-and-move-on weekly spelling list. Spelling words taught via effective instruction, a focused word list, and a repeating cycle of test-study-test are much more likely to become *permanent* in a student's mind. Our ability to spell is improved when we can remember the "look" of a word. Typically, this type of memorizing occurs when we see a word (and related words) many times through repeated exposure. Practice makes permanent, and specific types of instruction and word activities lend themselves to this achievement of permanency. A weekly routine of "memorize-and-move-on" does not.

Spelling Ability Develops from Excellent Instruction

How do we know that there is more to spelling than memorizing and recalling letter sequences? One piece of evidence comes from research that has shown that it is easier for children to remember predictable words than it is for them to remember irregular words (Treiman 1993). Think about it. If spelling were simply an act of memorizing, it should be just as easy for kids to memorize the spelling of irregular words, such as *want, does,* and *said,* as it is for them to spell more predictable words like *list, slap,* and *joke.* After all, they're all four-letter words.

But we know from experience that the first set of words (*want, does,* and *said*) is more problematic for children to spell. Some four-letter words are easier to spell than others! If your teaching career has been anything like mine, then you have seen more than your fair share of *wunt, duz,* and *sed.* If memorizing a letter sequence were all there was to it, then it should be just as easy for me to spell *silhouette* and *ricocheted* as it is for me to spell *cannonball* and *instruction* (all ten-letter words). In the interest of full disclosure, it took me three tries *with* my spell-checking program to spell *ricocheted. Cannonball* and *instruction* were not a problem. Spelling is difficult for me, so if I am really interested in learning how to spell *silhouette* accurately every time I write it, I should learn a strategy for remembering it and then practice employing that strategy as I spell the word multiple times.

Research has also shown that children have a limited visual memory for letter sequence. I was surprised to learn that when spelling, a child holds only two to three letters in sequence (Aaron, Wilcznski, and Keetay 1998). Thus, visual memory does not account for how our students spell four- and five-letter words, let alone multisyllabic words.

Because children don't typically spell by visually recalling a string of letters, memorizing a standardized weekly word list does little to help children learn *how* to spell. So what type of instruction *does* help kids learn how to spell? The most effective spelling instruction is

- systematic and sequential,
- direct and explicit (at times),
- focused and mastery based,
- differentiated,
- strategy based, and
- centered on sound, pattern, and meaning.

When we understand that instruction should be systematic and sequential, we know that powerful instruction leads to powerful learning. One type of powerful instruction is regularly and frequently following, in a thoughtful and planned way, a scope and sequence that provides children practice with hearing and spelling sounds, noticing and using patterns in words, and noticing and using the meaning parts of words at ever increasing levels of complexity.

When we understand that instruction should be direct and explicit at times, we recognize that powerful instruction is more than systematically teaching a spelling scope and sequence. It also involves techniques that directly and explicitly show sound-spelling relationships, such as telling and showing how the letter *f* stands for the *f* sound. In the later stages of spelling development, it means we use instruction to directly and explicitly teach children to notice, remember, and manipulate patterns and meaning, such as telling and showing them how *able*, *rifle*, and *bridle* are made up of open and consonant-*le* syllables, and how prefixes can be added to *able* to form new words that mean very different things, such as *unable* and *disable*.

When we understand that instruction should be focused and mastery based, we know that we should introduce only two to four spellings for a sound at a time, and that the introduction of sound spellings should unfold from the simple to the complex. Some basal programs introduce far too many sounds in one lesson. And if ten of our first-grade students have not mastered the spelling of short vowel sounds, then we should *not* move those students into the next set of spelling lessons that focus on long vowel sounds. Moving children, especially those in kindergarten, first, and second grades, too quickly through a spelling sequence leads to a lack of learning, a good deal of confusion, and the chance that guessing will become a habit. All of this can, in turn, lead to bigger problems in later grades. Our initial instruction should include many opportunities to slow down, step back, focus, reteach, and review, especially when we are teaching children who are in the early stages of spelling and reading development.

When we understand that instruction should be differentiated, we know that because there is a continuum of development and achievement in our classroom, a rigid one-size-fits-all spelling scope and sequence is not effective for all children. In November, in a classroom of twenty-two first-grade children, there may be ten who have not yet mastered the spelling of short vowel sounds. There may also be five children who easily spell short vowel sounds and are very capable of spelling multisyllabic words. This means we should consider providing different words and different types of instruction to two or even three groups of students.

When we understand that effective spelling instruction is strategy based, we know that spelling instruction should not lead children and parents to believe that the only way to spell a word is to memorize it and then recall it when it is needed for writing. Rather, we know that effective spelling instruction involves teaching students a number of different strategies, each of which can be used to spell practiced words correctly right off the bat, get as close to the correct spellings of unknown words as often as possible, and fix spelling mistakes, fine-tuning words that are "close" until they are exact.

When we understand that spelling instruction should be centered on sound, pattern, and meaning, we know that spelling instruction should *not* lead children to believe that words are strings of letters that can be memorized through a classroom activity that sounds like this: "The word is *dumbfound*. Spell it! D-U-M-B-F-O-U-N-D! The word is *diphthong*. Spell it! D-I-P-H-T-H-O-N-G! The word is *discombobulated*. Spell it! D-I-S-C . . ." You get the idea.

Rather, we know that spelling is orthography, which is coming up with a correct sequence of letters to create a specific word through a process that involves hearing sounds and assigning letters to them, thinking in terms of patterns found in words, and always cross-checking what we hear and see with what the word means. Thus, our instruction leads students to understand that they can spell by listening to the sounds of a word and then applying single letters and groups of letters to each sound. Our instruction also teaches children that they can spell by remembering and applying letter patterns (or word families), such as *–an*, *-ight*, and *–all*, as well as inflectional endings such as *–ing* and *–ed* and common prefixes and suffixes like *dis-*, *pre-*, *-tion*, and *–able*. And our instruction teaches children, both younger and older, to pay attention to meaning as they spell.

Morphology is an important aspect of spelling, and it is helpful to teach children to identify and analyze the structure of English's linguistic units, such as morphemes, root words, and parts of speech. When younger children get in the habit of thinking about meaning, they are more likely to spell homophones correctly, as in the sentence "*Their* dog was somewhere out *there*, lost in the forest," or correctly spell the *t* sound at the end of a past-tense verb as *–ed*, as in the words *helped, fussed,* and *plopped*. Older children can use meaning to correctly spell words related in spelling through meaning but differing in pronunciation (such as *define, definite,* and *definition*), as well as spell words that share similar sounds but are unrelated in meaning (such as *adept* and *adapt* or *excel* and *accelerate*).

Spelling Is Developmental

For me, literacy is a fascinating blend of art and science. I delight in practicing the art of motivating kids or getting a complex concept across to a group of eager students. I also love exploring the many theories that populate the field of literacy, such as constructivism or reading as a transactional process. These theories—studied, debated, and discussed over many decades—allow me to move beyond intuition to a place where I can logically and scientifically understand how and why literacy skills develop in children. From there I can better understand how and when to use particular classroom instructional practices.

To help us better understand what we see in our student spellers and how we might best instruct them, let's consider the theory of spelling development. When we understand that spelling is developmental, we know that *all* children acquire knowledge in stages that have to do with sounds, letter patterns, and meaning. As Marcia Invernizzi says in *No More Phonics and Spelling Worksheets*, "[A]ll students learning to read and write English experience these same developmental trajectories" (Palmer and Invernizzi 2015, 22). But although students experience the same paths of knowledge acquisition and skill development, different students travel these paths at naturally varying rates of speed. For this reason, we can expect to see varying levels of spelling achievement in a classroom, and we can begin to understand why a one-size-fits-all spelling program is less than effective.

Spelling development also varies according to our ability to effectively teach students. At the start of every year, we can expect a variety of achievement levels. But as the year progresses, if some students are achieving but others aren't, it may be because of inappropriate instruction. I say *may* because there are, of course, many factors outside of school that affect student learning. But we can't discount our own instruction. There's no doubt that some instructional practices bring forth surges of achievement and others promote only modest or minimal gains.

Knowing that spelling is developmental means knowing that the mistakes students make on their spelling quizzes and in their authentic writing are not random or bizarre actions (as I once thought), but merely attempts to apply the knowledge they currently have about how spelling works. It takes a trained eye and a certain amount of knowledge to understand where students lie on the continuum of spelling development. But when we correctly place students on that spelling continuum, we are in a much better position to craft instruction that enables them to achieve.

Spelling ability develops simultaneously, harmoniously, and integrally with reading ability and writing ability. We can think of the concurrent, evolving nature of these literacy abilities as the "Synchrony of Literacy Development," a term coined by Donald Bear and his colleagues and rooted in decades of research by the likes of Edmund Henderson, James Beers, Jean Chall, Linnea Ehri,

The Concurrent and Interrelated Nature of Literacy Development

	3 to 5 Pre-K	5 to 6 Late K–Early First	6 to 7 Early/Mid-First–Early/Mid-Second	7 to 9 Early/Late Second–Early Fourth	9 to 13 Early Fourth–Late Eighth
Typical Age and Grade Level of Child					
Layers of Orthography	Alphabet/Sound		Pattern		Meaning
Reading Stages	Emergent Pretend Reading	Beginning	Transitional	Intermediate to Advanced	
		Alphabetic principle takes hold; word-by-word reading; some stamina	Fluency takes hold; prosody developing; greater stamina	Fluency, prosody, vocabulary, and comprehension all expand; concentration and stamina increase; many genres are explored; reading styles develop	
Writing Stages	Emergent Pretend Writing	Beginning	Transitional	Intermediate to Advanced	
		"Ideas as words" takes hold; few sentences written	Greater mechanical fluency and organization; paragraphs develop	Writing fluency, vocabulary, and expression of ideas all expand; many genres are explored; writing style and voice develop	
Spelling Stages (Upper row based on work of Gentry, lower two on work of Bear et al.)	Precommunicative	Semiphonetic	Phonetic	Transitional	Conventional or Correct
	Emergent	Letter Name/Alphabetic	Patterns Within Words	Syllables and Affixes	Derivational Relations
	Early Middle Late	Early Middle Late	Early Middle Late	Early Middle Late	Early Middle Late

Figure 1.3 The concurrent and interrelated nature of literacy development

Louisa Moats, Richard Gentry, and others. Figure 1.3 shows the interrelatedness of spelling, writing, and reading, as well as the concurrent nature of their development; I've adapted this chart from *Words Their Way* (Bear et al. 2012, 19) and incorporated additional information from my study of the research noted above.

Figure 1.4 shows kindergarten writing done in mid-October. This student is developing the ability to spell based on letters and sounds. He is also using a magic line to represent unfamiliar words, as well as using words in the room to try to spell words like *the* and *it*.

Figure 1.5 shows a piece of midyear third-grade writing. This student shows a mixture of spelling development stages: she is able to correctly use patterns and apply endings in some multisyllabic words but not in others. She also recognizes many of her misspelled words and is using strategies to correct them.

While looking over the figures, keep these two important things in mind: First, spelling ability typically develops at a slower rate than reading ability because it is not uncommon for a second grader to easily read words such as *before* or *question*, yet not be able to spell them correctly while writing. Second, the stages of spelling development tend to overlap, just like the developmental stages of reading and writing do. Nothing in teaching is ever simple, right? Understanding literacy development is an exercise in combining book-learned facts and knowledge with the experience that you gain from working with children. Thus, deep understanding takes a certain amount of time.

Coming Up

Now that we know that spelling is more than a list and a test, let's put our knowledge to work and begin taking steps toward differentiated and developmental spelling instruction that teaches children how to spell, not what to spell. In Chapter 2, we'll look at how to conduct quick and easy diagnostic assessments at the beginning of the year. These assessments will accomplish a number of things, including providing information on the overall "spelling health" of your class, pointing out the developmental stages of individual students, and offering possibilities for formative assessment as you move forward in the year. We will also discuss current thinking around the weekly spelling list and test, to see how these components of a traditional spelling program fit with other aspects of best practice in literacy instruction.

Figure 1.4 Kindergarten writing: sound-letter spelling stage

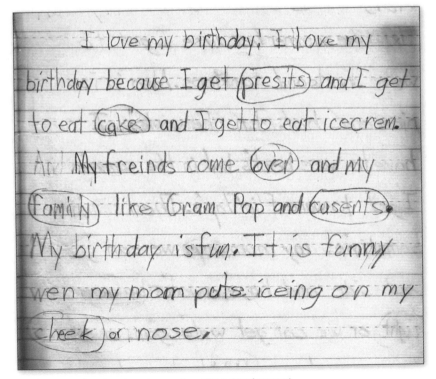

Figure 1.5 Overlapping stages of spelling development

Before moving on to the next chapter, I encourage you to reflect on the questions below. I've included them to help you connect the ideas and practices described in each chapter to your own ideas about spelling content and classroom instruction. Instructional transformation comes about through a cycle of learning, reflection, mindful application, and practice, and I hope these questions promote that cycle.

EXPLORE CONNECTIONS

1. Think about how you teach spelling, reading, and writing. Do you explicitly and directly connect them? If so, how? Is there room to make even stronger, more explicit connections?

2. Think about the developmental nature of spelling. Now go back and look at Figures 1.4 and 1.5. What do the spelling errors in these writing pieces tell you? What do the correct spellings tell you? Where on the continuum of spelling development do these students lie?

3. Reflect on the scope, sequence, and rate of delivery of your spelling and phonics instruction. Are there opportunities for true differentiation? Does the curriculum dictate that you move on, week to week, even if some of your students have not mastered the patterns and concepts of the week? What are the ramifications of this for writing? For reading?

CHAPTER 2

Assess Spelling Knowledge

IN THIS CHAPTER

- We consider a beginning-of-the-year assessment plan and then explore the assessments that make up the plan. Assessment options consist of a spelling inventory, a phonics inventory, and a student's writing sample. These assessments can be used diagnostically and formatively, and to assess growth against benchmarks.

- We discuss how spelling inventories and writing samples help us understand the range of spelling development in a classroom. Once we understand the range of development, we can plan for instruction that brings about better reading, writing, and spelling.

- Finally, we begin to explore how a well-constructed weekly word list anchors an effective program of instruction. This program of instruction includes differentiation, activities that teach how to spell (not what to spell), and a test-study-test cycle that is more formative in nature than summative.

The Year Begins

Picture this: it's a late-summer morning, and twenty-two excited second graders file into your classroom to begin their second week of school. They are still learning your classroom routines, and you are still learning their personalities and quirks. But you have begun spelling instruction that will help lead these students to independent reading, writing, and spelling. Yes, you have big plans.

This year, you want to focus and differentiate your word lists, draw attention to letter patterns, provide a bit more time for word study activities, reteach lessons that aren't mastered the first time around, and teach strategies that students can use independently to solve spelling problems while writing. But before you do any of this, you want to assess your students' general spelling knowledge. Here is your plan:

- Early in the school year, you will give every student a **primary elementary spelling inventory**. This will be given to the whole group and will take approximately fifteen to twenty minutes.

- As a follow-up, and when you have a moment, you will give any child who scored above 90 percent on the primary inventory the first half of an **intermediate elementary spelling inventory**.

- Within the first two weeks of school, you will have each child produce an **independent writing sample**. This will take twenty to twenty-five minutes. First you will help the students brainstorm a topic list of what they can write about (school, friends, a favorite pet, swimming at the Y, and so on). Next, you'll give them uninterrupted time to write, perhaps ten to fifteen minutes. During this time, you will motivate them with praise, but you'll refrain from helping them (unless a child is totally stuck) and you won't offer solutions to spelling problems or tell anyone how to spell unknown words.

- Next, as your guided reading groups get up and running, or as your whole-group reading routines take shape, you will give all or some of your students a **phonics inventory**. Because the inventory is a one-on-one assessment and takes three or four minutes to give to each student, you plan to enlist the help of a Title I teacher or trained literacy assistant. After the inventory is given, you plan to compare its results with the same child's spelling inventory and writing sample.

This beginning-of-the-year assessment plan is a solid one. It will give you a broad yet rich overview of your students' spelling and writing abilities, as well as insight into their reading ability. The data it produces will give you ideas about what spelling, writing, and decoding skills need to be addressed in the upcoming months and will help you map the first months of instruction. Finally, the scores from these assessments will serve as the first step of a benchmark plan, because when you gather scores early in the school year, you can compare them with scores from mid-January and late April, efficiently monitoring your students' progress toward goals even as you continue to pinpoint problem areas.

Each assessment in this beginning-of-the-year plan has merit and will bring important literacy information to light. In the following sections we'll look at how and why each one can play a part in transforming traditional spelling instruction.

Spelling Inventories

Spelling inventories are "big picture" assessments designed to give information about students' broad knowledge of orthography, which is the spelling system of our English language. They provide information on students' ability to make use of the alphabetic principle, remember and use conventional spelling patterns, and apply word meaning, all in service of committing a multitude of words to the "dictionaries in their brains" and spelling words correctly as they write.

Spelling inventories are terrifically useful. First, they are a relatively easy way to gain information about your students' understanding of how words are spelled. Second, they can be the first step toward breaking free of a one-size-fits-all spelling program. Once you give a spelling inventory and see that distinct levels of spelling knowledge exist in your class, you'll want to begin differentiating your content and instruction.

Because spelling inventories provide diagnostic information, they can also be used to plan intervention groups. When shared with a reading specialist, a spelling inventory's information can guide small-group instruction. For example, you might find that five of your third-grade students have not mastered the hearing, reproduction, and spelling of the short *a*, *i*, and *e* sounds. Knowing this, a reading specialist or a speech/language instructor could take these children aside and teach them the skill.

Finally, spelling inventories give more than just information about spelling. They also provide insight into students' overall reading and writing achievement. Marcia Invernizzi writes, "[Q]ualitative spelling inventories assess children's developmental spelling knowledge that in large measure determines the quality of their reading and writing" (Palmer and Invernizzi 2015, 17). In other words, spelling inventories go a long way toward explaining how and why children read and write as they do.

Word Features

Spelling inventories are lists of words, typically ordered from easiest to most difficult to spell. Each word is chosen carefully to demonstrate specific aspects of orthography. These aspects are called word features. Inventories designed for younger children focus on word features that develop early on, such as short vowel sounds; consonant digraphs such as *ch, sh,* and *ck* and inflectional endings (letters added to change the forms of nouns, verbs, and adjectives) such as *es*, *ed*, and *ing*. Inventories for older children concentrate on word features typically mastered later in life, such as variant vowel spellings (*ow, ai, oi*), prefixes such as *dis* and *ab*, and Latin roots such as *vis*, *fus*, and *quo*.

Figures 2.1 and 2.2 show snippets of two spelling inventories I developed for this book. In Figure 2.1 you'll see that the words are made up of one or more of the following word features: beginning, middle, and ending consonants; short vowels; consonant blends; and consonant digraphs. The words listed in Figure 2.2 are constructed of different features: *r*-controlled syllables, variant vowels, prefixes, suffixes, and Latin roots.

Word Feature ➜	Consonants			Short Vowel	Consonant Digraph	Consonant Blends
	Begin	Mid	End			
1. set	s		t	e		
2. mob	m		b	o		
3. dip	d		p	i		
4. hug	h		g	u		
5. flash				a	sh	fl
6. slick					ck	sl
7. hill			ll			
8. mess			ss			

Figure 2.1 Word features: Primary Long-Form Spelling Inventory

Word Feature ➜	R control	Other/variant vowels	Special consonant	Prefix	Suffix	Roots
confusion				con	ion	fus
invisible			s	in	ible	vis
disappearance		schwa a		dis	ance	appear
quotient					ent	quot
judgment			dg		ment	judg
pleasure					ure	pleas
naturally	ur				al-ly	nat

Figure 2.2 Word features: Intermediate Long-Form Spelling Inventory

When we look at words from the perspective of features, we understand that children who spell an unstudied word correctly know how to control its specific word features or have already committed the whole word to their brain dictionary. Conversely, children who misspell the word either totally lack control of a feature or have some semblance of understanding but are using the feature in an incorrect way. For the purposes of scoring a spelling inventory and understanding a child's control (or lack thereof), we typically say that when a feature is missed in *two or more words*, the child does not have control of using that feature.

Which Inventory to Choose?

There are many inventories to pick from, including Richard Gentry's *Monster Test* (2007), Sylvia Green's *Primary and Elementary Word Analysis* (2016), and the *Qualitative Spelling Inventories* that appear in the *Words Their Way* program (Bear et al. 2012). Also, basal reading programs (such as McGraw-Hill's *Wonders*) increasingly include spelling inventories as part of their assessment package, so if you use a published reading series, look to see if it has a spelling inventory.

Because I want you to have everything you need to be successful, I created spelling inventories for this book. One, which I call the Short-Form Inventory, draws its inspiration from the *Phonics Screening Inventory* published by the Florida Center for Reading Research (Florida Department of Education 2009) as well as from Sylvia Green's *Informal Word Analysis Inventory* (2016). My Short Form Inventory comes in two flavors, one for younger children (primary elementary) and one for older children (intermediate elementary). My other inventory, which I call the Long Form, is modeled on a more complex format. Figures 2.1 and 2.2 are pieces of these two more complex inventories. You'll find each reproduced in its entirety in Appendix A of this book, as well as under the File Cabinet tab of my website, www.MarkWeaklandLiteracy.com.

If you are familiar with spelling theory, are comfortable with collecting and managing lots of data, and want to understand each student on a refined level, then choose a more complex inventory like my Long Form. If you are new to spelling features or have never used a spelling inventory before, then start with the *Phonics Screening Inventory* from the Florida Center for Reading Research or use the Short Form of my spelling inventory (and use the classroom scoring form, not the individual student form). Regardless of which inventory you start with, you can always move to a more or less complex one that fits your level of background knowledge and comfort.

Giving a Spelling Inventory

Although it's not within the scope of this book to instruct you in all the particulars of scoring and analyzing a specific spelling inventory, I can offer some general suggestions, starting with how to give the assessment.

Before giving the inventory, make sure that the majority of your students will produce enough misspelled words to analyze. In other words, don't pick an inventory that will produce only one or two misspelled words. You *want* kids to miss words, because student errors tell you which spelling skills need further instruction.

On the other hand, there is no need to push students into an inventory that will be frustrating. Also, there is no need to finish giving an entire inventory if the majority of your students are generating errors within the first ten to fifteen sample items. In general, an inventory marked *primary elementary* should work for typically achieving students in first, second, and third grade. An inventory marked *intermediate elementary* might work well for more advanced third graders, and it should be appropriate for typically achieving fourth, fifth, and sixth graders.

When you give an inventory, let your students know they will be spelling words that they haven't studied, and be sure to tell them they are not taking a test. I typically say something like, "I am giving you a list of words to spell that you have not studied before. This is not a test, and it will not be graded. So don't worry if you don't know how to spell the word. Just do your best! Try to spell each word as best you can. Seeing *how* you spell helps me plan our spelling lessons for the year. If you don't know how to spell a word, try using a strategy to help you spell it."

After my little speech, I treat the inventory like a traditional spelling test. I arrange the kids so they won't be tempted to copy. I pass out a half-sheet of paper and have the kids write their names and the date. I say the spelling words naturally. I give a sentence for each word, and I repeat the word after I say the sentence. I keep the pace brisk. The authors of some inventories recommend that children in kindergarten and early first grade receive the test in small groups. Remember, you don't need to give the entire inventory. For example, at the start of the year in first grade, you might want to give the first fifteen words of a primary elementary spelling inventory. Or at the start of the year in third grade, you can give the first twenty words of an intermediate elementary spelling inventory.

Scoring and Analyzing a Spelling Inventory

Once you have administered, collected, and reviewed the student responses, group the papers into three piles: a pile for papers with few errors (zero to four on the entire inventory), a pile with a moderate number of errors (perhaps five to ten), and a pile with a high number of errors (maybe eleven or more). What you consider to be a low number or a high number will vary, based on the performance of your class.

Once you have grouped the papers, look for trends both within the groupings and across the groupings. Consider both correctly spelled words and incorrectly spelled words. Knowing that two or more errors in any feature category typically means that a student has not mastered control of that feature, try to discern what your students know and don't know about word features. Ask yourself these types of questions:

- Do my students spell consonants correctly?

- Do they correctly spell digraphs (for example, *ch, ck, th, sh*) and blends (for example, *bl, cr, str*)?

- Did they have control of *short vowel* sounds?

- Do they misspell *long vowel* sounds? If so, are the errors clustered in any feature category, such as *vowel-consonant-e* words, *open syllables* (for example, *fla, tu),* or *common long vowel teams* (for example, *ai, ay, oa, ee*)?

- Do my students misspell r-*controlled vowel* sounds (such as *ar, or, ur, ir*)?

- What percentage of my students missed two or more spellings of the less-common vowel teams, such as *ow, aw,* or *oi*?

- Which students have control of inflectional endings (such as *ing, ed, es*)?

- Do they know how to spell across syllable junctures (such as *nn* in *pennies, tt* in *battle*)?

- Have they developed control over prefixes and suffixes (for example, *de, ab, in, ible, able*)?

- Do my students know how to spell multisyllabic words based on roots (for example, *fus, quo, judg*)?

- Do they accurately use multiple affixes?

- Are my students exhibiting any trends not specified on the inventory, such as a reversing *b*s and *d*s or showing poorly formed letters?

The final step of your analysis is to discern what word features your students need instruction on. If you give the inventory at the beginning of the year, you can use the information immediately. If you give it at the end of the year, next year's teacher can use the information. For example, in May 2015 I gave a twenty-six-word primary spelling inventory (from *Words Their Way* by Bear et al. 2012) to a group of thirty-two second graders. Information from this group of second graders would be valuable to a third-grade teacher planning for his or her 2016–17 spelling instruction.

By the way, these thirty-two children were thought to be a large group of "middle of the road" achievers. But in fact, they were *not* achieving in a similar fashion. Rather, they were bunched into small groups across the spectrum of spelling development, some with great control over most spelling features and some with little control.

As a teacher, you want to know the individual spelling achievements of your students so that you can teach needed spelling skills at the individual or small-group level, if at all possible. Children who have little control over age-appropriate spelling features (such as beginning third graders who are still confusing short vowel spellings with consonant–vowel–e spellings) are at risk for failure in both reading and writing. The only way to truly help these kids master critical encoding and decoding skills is to scale back content to their instructional level and then provide them with repeated practice. One way to do this is to create two or three small groups that will receive differentiated content and possibly differentiated instruction.

Figure 2.3 shows three spelling inventories from three individuals in the group of second graders. You can see the wide range of spelling development, from the child on the right, who has control of all the spelling features presented in the inventory, to the child on the left, who is still developing control of many features.

After grouping the inventories from the thirty-two second graders (I grouped the papers into four piles, not three) and reflecting on the scores, I came up with this rough analysis:

- Nine students (28 percent) made zero to two errors. Any errors these students made involved inflectional endings (adding *s* and *es* to nouns to make them plural, adding *ed* and *ing* to verbs to change their tense).

- Four students (13 percent) made four to five errors. Their errors involved vowel teams (especially lower-frequency teams such as *oi* and *ir*) or inflectional endings.

1. fan	1 fan	1 fan
2. pet	2 pet	2 pet
3. dig	3 dig	3 dig
4. robe	4 rob	4 rob
5. hope	5 hope	5 hope
6. what	6 wait	6 wait
7. gum	7 gum	7 gum
8. sleid	8 sled	8 sled
9. stick	9 stick	9 stick
10. shine	10 shine	10 shine
11. drem	11 dream	11 dream
12. blade	12 blade	12 blade
13. couch	13 coach	13 coach
14. frite	14 Fright	14 fright
15. chood	15 chud	15 chewed
16. crale	16 crawl	16 crawl
17. wishes	17 Wishes	17 wishes
18. thorn	18 thorn	18 thorn
19. shouted	19 shoted	19 shouted
20. spoily	20 spoil	20 spoil
21. grovel	21 growl	21 growl
22. thered	22 thicried	22 third
23.		23 camped
24		24 tries
25.		25 clapping

Figure 2.3 Spelling inventories from three second graders

- Ten students (31 percent) made seven to ten errors. Their errors involved vowel teams (especially *oi* and *ir*) and inflectional endings.

- Nine (28 percent) made fourteen or more errors. Their errors included digraph *ck* (spelled *k*), vowel-consonant-e (*shin* for *shine*; *blad* for *blade*), other long vowels (*what* and *wate* for *wait*, *coch* for *coach*), lower-frequency vowel teams (*oi*), and inflectional endings.

Two things stood out for me: (1) the bulk of the group needed instruction on inflectional endings and lower-frequency vowel teams, and (2) almost one-third of the group was not in control of long vowel spellings. If I was a teacher looping with these students, or if I was a third-grade teacher inheriting these students in the fall, I would plan for the following lessons:

1. I would start with a review of short vowel spellings, making sure to explicitly and directly instruct on what a closed syllable is (CVC or VC word) and what sounds are associated with the vowels in these patterns. Into this, I'd fold instruction on the *ck* digraph (showing how it appears only at the end of a word, how it typically appears at the end of a one-syllable word rather than a multisyllabic word, and so on). For children who didn't need this review because they were in control of these word features, I'd differentiate my lesson by giving them a different word list to study or different spelling activities to engage in.

2. After the review of short vowel spellings, I'd run a lesson that compares the short vowel-sound syllable (closed) with the vowel-consonant-*e* (VC*e*) syllable. And I'd combine this lesson with a review of how to add inflectional endings to "silent *e*" words, making sure that the students were mastering the "drop *e*" convention. Once again, for children who had mastered these word features, I'd differentiate with different word lists or instruction.

3. After spending a week on the vowel-consonant-*e* feature and the "drop *e*" convention for inflectional endings (*ed* and *ing*), I'd look at my formative assessment data. If more than three or four of my twenty-four students still hadn't mastered how to spell *rod* and *rode, plan* and *plane,* and *slide* and *sliding,* I'd teach a VC*e* lesson one more time.

4. Finally, only after I'd determined that 90 percent or more of the kids were in control of the short vowel, vowel-consonant-*e*, and "drop *e*" features would I move on to teaching the scope and sequence traditionally found in third-grade programs: *r*-controlled syllables (for example, *ir, ar, or, ore*), long vowel teams (such as *oa, ee, ea, igh, ay, ai*), and variant vowel teams (*ow, ou, oi, oy,* and so on).

I believe that giving a spelling inventory is one of the most powerful first steps you can take in transforming any nondifferentiated spelling program. Also, giving a spelling inventory helps a teacher in any type of reading program—from basal to balanced literacy to reading workshop—understand his or her students' encoding and decoding abilities more deeply. So if you haven't given a spelling inventory in the past, I encourage you to give one within the first ten days of the school year. If you are reading this book toward the middle or end of the school year, find an inventory and give it now. The goal is to get started.

I also encourage you to take your spelling inventory to one or two like-minded teachers and form a study group. Make this study part of your yearly professional development, part of your student learning objectives, or part of your action research. With a study group, you can collaborate to answer any questions that arise, and you can bounce ideas back and forth about how you might change your spelling, phonics, and writing instruction based on the results.

Phonics Inventories

Because phonics (decoding) is the flip side of spelling (encoding), we can say that phonics inventories are the flip side of spelling inventories. In fact, some inventories, such as one from the Florida Center for Reading Research, are explicitly designed to assess both sides of the coin. You can give the word list as a spelling inventory (you read the word and the child writes it) or you can give it as a phonics inventory (the child reads the word and you write down what she says). Comparing information from a phonics inventory with information from a spelling inventory helps you understand literacy development holistically. It's not just about how students spell; it's also about how they read, and vice versa.

When I was a reading specialist, I gave the CORE Phonics Survey three times a year. The survey comes from the book *Assessing Reading: Multiple Measures* (Diamond 2008), which includes a number of useful assessments, such as a phoneme segmentation assessment, a high-frequency word survey, and oral reading fluency measures. I like the CORE Phonics Survey because it is easy to give, comprehensive, easy to score, and contains both real words and pseudo-words. There are, of course, other phonics inventories to choose from. Earlier I mentioned that newer basal programs often have spelling inventories in their assessment package. This is also true for phonics inventories, which can be found in reading programs published by Houghton Mifflin Harcourt, Scott-Foresman, and others. Also, some school districts create their own informal instruments.

Unlike a spelling inventory, a phonics inventory must be administered to students individually. If you give one to every child in your classroom, it'll eat up a big chunk of time. But you don't have to give the assessment to every child.

Use a phonics survey in a more targeted fashion by selecting the students you are most concerned about and then giving the survey only to them.

Figure 2.4 shows one section of a hypothetical phonics survey score sheet. This example is similar to an actual assessment, the CORE Phonics Survey, which contains twelve sections. In a phonics survey, a student reads from lists of words and possibly pseudo-words until the teacher tells him or her to stop. As the student reads, the teacher notes errors on the score sheet. Typically, each word is simply scored right or wrong. But when you become more skillful at giving the inventory, you will be better able to note exactly what the student says (similar to writing words on a fluency measure or running record). Later, you can analyze the errors.

R-controlled vowels					
Score					
/5	surf	fern	corn	shirt	farm
/5	form	pert	smart	hurl	firm
/5	lirt	serm	gorn	larf	jurt
/15					

Figure 2.4 Section of an example phonics survey

Phonics surveys typically have cutoff scores, sometimes for the entire survey as well as for each section, that signal a need for instruction (or not). For example, in a section like the one shown in Figure 2.4 a score of 14/15 is considered to be benchmark level. If the child scores 10/15 to 13/15, he or she needs instruction. A score of 9/15 and below tells you that the child needs intensive instruction.

Gathering information on how a student encodes and decodes enables you to determine if he or she is having difficulty with the same features in both reading and spelling. For example, you might notice that a fourth-grade student who misspells words containing an *r*-controlled syllable (for example, *desrving* for *deserving* and *flaivr* for *flavor*) also consistently misreads the *r*-controlled words on a phonics inventory (for example, reading *fun* for *fern* and *pet* for *pert*). If this is the case, it's safe to say this student needs explicit and systematic instruction in *r*-controlled phonics and spelling patterns.

Writing Samples

Like spelling inventories, writing samples provide "big picture" information. When viewed through the lens of assessment, uncorrected student writing samples give information on how students hear and spell the sounds of the English language, use the rules of our grammatical system, and apply meaning as they write words and craft sentences. By examining the spelling errors in independent writing samples and cross-referencing them with the errors seen on spelling and phonics inventories, you can gain a clearer picture of a child's specific stage of reading and writing development.

Let's take a look at two independent writing samples from third graders. In Figure 2.5, we see a boy who can spell many word features, is confused in his spelling of other word features, and is occasionally spelling words in a way that mirrors his dialect. Specifically, this student has control of many features seen in two-syllable words, including the *ect* ending (*direct* and *collect*), plurals (*workers* and *reasons*), the consonant-*le* syllable (*peple*), and the *r*-controlled syllable in some words (*boring* and *workers)*. Meanwhile, he has some confusion about patterns, including the spelling of long vowels (*pant* for *paint*). Finally, to me it is no surprise that he has spelled *direct* as *drect* and *collect* as *clect*, because in western Pennsylvania, where this boy lives, people tend to collapse two-syllable words into one.

In general, this boy's writing sample tells me that he is developing the ability to spell two- and three-syllable words, he is ready for instruction and practice with vowel-team and *r*-controlled vowel patterns, and he could use a brushing-up on what a vowel "says" when it is within a closed syllable.

In Figure 2.6, we see a girl who is developmentally behind the boy. Many of her short vowel sound words are spelled correctly. She has control of *er* at the end of words, and she hears many of the sounds in most words and can assign the correct letters and letter combinations. But she lacks knowledge of what the Wilson Reading System calls the "bonus letter," which is the convention of doubling the letter *l*, *s*, or *f* when the sound occurs at the end of one-syllable short vowel words, such as *pass, tell, fuss, stiff,* and *fluff*. Also, she has not mastered vowel-team and *r*-controlled vowel patterns, which we can see when she writes

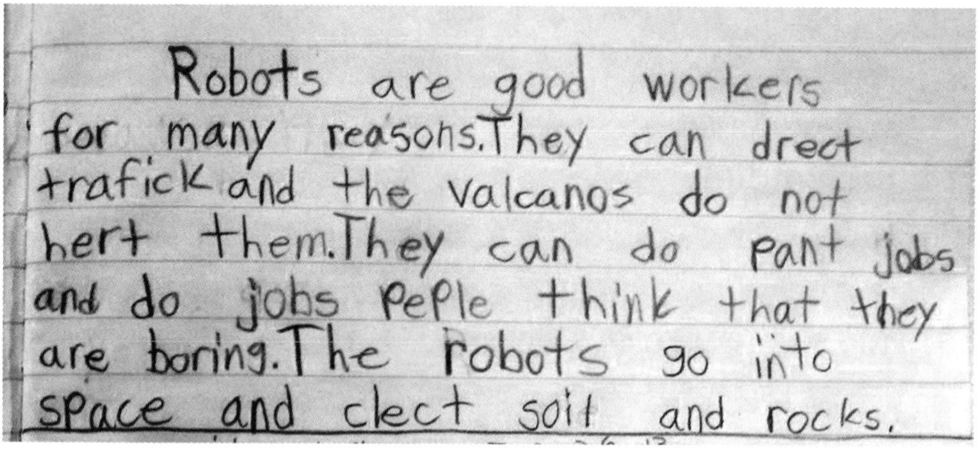

> Robots are good workers for many reasons. They can drect trafick and the valcanos do not hert them. They can do pant jobs and do jobs peple think that they are boring. The robots go into space and clect soil and rocks.

Robots are good workers for many reasons. They can drect trafick and the valcanos do not hert them. They can do pant jobs and do jobs peple think that they are boring. The robots go into space and clect soil and rocks.

Figure 2.5 More advanced spelling development

clen for *clean, porck* for *park,* and *tercher* for *teacher.* Finally, I'd say she is not employing the strategy of "stretching out" a word, writing letters for the sounds in a word and then cross-checking spelling and sounds. Thus, the word *friends* lacks a letter for the *r* sound, and *pencil* lacks a letter for the *l* sound.

Before we move on, I must admit that I really enjoy reading student writing. I find most pieces to be full of immediacy, creativity, and charm. Not only do they give me a window into the lives of students, but they remind me of my own childhood. Reading student writing, however, is more than a personal pleasure. Student writing shows me what kids know about vocabulary, grammar, style, and spelling. If writing pieces are produced regularly, they make for ready-made formative assessments. As you look over a student's writing, pick one or two features to focus on, be it short vowel patterns, *r*-controlled vowel patterns, or

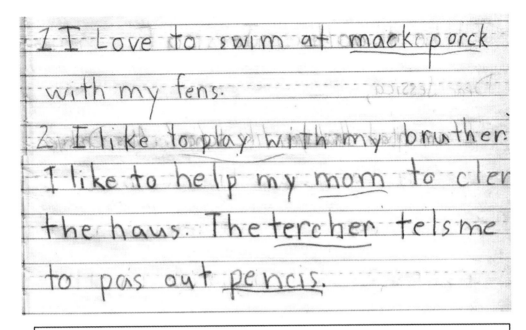

Figure 2.6 Less advanced spelling development

inflectional endings, and track them over a nine-week period, week by week. When your word-level instruction is working, you will see a gradual decrease in the number of mistakes in this feature, an increase in the number of close-to-correctly-spelled words, and attempts to spell more sophisticated and multisyllabic words.

The Weekly Spelling List and the Test-Study-Test Cycle

So far we have touched upon three forms of assessment: benchmark, diagnostic, and formative. We have yet to talk about summative assessment, and there's a reason for that. When it comes to teaching children how to read and write, the traditional summative testing cycle (aka "memorize and move on") is ineffective. On the other hand, a carefully constructed word list combined with effective instruction and a test-study-test cycle (which includes a pre-test at the beginning of the week) helps children become better readers and writers. I am *not* here to tell you to get rid of the weekly spelling list and test. I am, however, asking you to create a more instructionally relevant weekly word list; to change your assessment routine to include a pre-test that leads to some type of differentiation; to think of your post-test as a formative test, not a summative one; and to realize that everything you do in spelling, including your end-of-the-week test, can be an opportunity to instruct children on how to read and write.

To get a better picture of what I am talking about, let's take a trip to Mr. C's second-grade classroom, where I recently taught a series of twenty-minute spelling lessons. These lessons begin to demonstrate how to differentiate instruction; infuse lessons with words for writing; provide students with opportunities to read, write, and spell many words built from a limited number of patterns; and use activities that teach children *how* to spell, not what to spell.

Mr. C and I started by modifying a word list he typically gives to students in the fourth marking period. The original list was made up of words spelled in three different ways, and it included the words *adhere, reindeer,* and *cashmere.* After changing the list to focus on two spelling patterns rather than three, and after replacing words like *adhere* and *cashmere* with words that second graders might actually use while writing (such as *year, steer,* and *nearly*), we gave the children a pre-test of twelve words on Monday.

Analysis of the pre-test provided few surprises, especially when viewed in light of what Mr. C knew about his students as readers and writers. About two-thirds of the class had a good start on knowing which words use the *eer* spelling and which ones use the *ear* spelling. According to Mr. C, these children were also his better readers and writers. The other third of the class had little to no control of *eer/ear* spellings or the *ly* ending. *Cheer* was spelled *chear,* and *nearly* was spelled *neerly, neree,* and *nerlee.*

Based on the pre-test results, we constructed two fifteen-word spelling lists for students to use throughout the week. One list was basic, one more advanced.

Most important, the word lists were tools for organizing our instruction—not the reason for our instruction. In other words, rather than giving students words to memorize, we were using words to help the students build strategies for spelling unknown words, to expand the dictionaries in their brains, and to develop their reading and writing skills.

The instruction Mr. C and I provided was mostly large group, but one day we worked with small groups. Throughout the week we did quick but effective spelling activities, including word sorts, "Look Touch Say" reading, and dictation with instant error correction. On Thursday we allowed the kids to do a buddy study. In each of these activities, students used, studied, and spelled words on their take-home list, but they also used, studied, and spelled words that weren't on their list. These words had to be spelled by using strategies and knowledge of how words work. Everything mentioned in this section, from pre-test and strategy instruction to differentiated word lists and spelling activities like Look Touch Say and buddy study (which are fully explained in Chapter 6), can be easily implemented in a balanced literacy or workshop model of reading instruction. Because the frameworks of balanced literacy and reading and writing workshop are wonderfully flexible and expandable, they can easily accommodate the spelling ideas mentioned here and in upcoming chapters.

On Friday we gave two versions of a post-test. Each version tested ten of the fifteen words the kids had on their formal lists. Because Mr. C was new to giving two word lists to one group of students, I modeled the procedure. Our test consisted of just ten words because we wanted to think of the Friday test as a formative test, dipping down to check on instruction, rather than a summative test that eats up a lot of class time, takes more time to grade, and gives the same type of information as the shorter test, only more of it.

To wrap this up, there is nothing wrong with a weekly spelling list and a weekly spelling test. Weekly spelling lists and tests enable a number of best practices, including differentiation, the test-study-test cycle, and the gathering of formative data. Also, there is nothing wrong with sending a spelling list home for children to study. Parents like the idea of a take-home list because they had one when they were kids and because helping their children study a word list is typically something they feel comfortable doing. And although you may engage in this traditional practice (giving a weekly spelling list to take home), you can still consider yourself to be transitioning to a progressive way of thinking (spelling is developmental, lists are differentiated, children are taught how to spell, not what to spell). Regarding weekly spelling lists and tests, the important points to remember are that (1) a spelling list should be in service of your instruction, and (2) your instruction should be leading children to understand *how* to spell, not what to spell.

Assessment and Chronically Misspelled Writing Words

Before we end this chapter, let's explore the relationship among the weekly spelling list, the writing that students regularly do, and the words that some students chronically misspell when they write.

Some kindergarten and first-grade teachers use a literacy framework that holistically addresses the developmental aspects of reading, writing, and spelling. Here I am thinking of balanced literacy and workshop frameworks. If you walked into a classroom based on one of these frameworks, you would certainly see sections of walls devoted to words that students can use in their writing (see Figures 2.7a and 2.7b). When students are given instruction and tools that enable them to solve their writing and spelling problems, as well as multiple opportunities to correctly spell "tricky" or "outlaw" spelling words in writing, they are likely to spell these words correctly in future writing in the upper grades.

But if children aren't given opportunities to practice self-monitoring and use self-correction tools, they may begin to chronically misspell words when writing. What do I mean by chronically misspelled words? Here I mean reoccurring

Figures 2.7a (Above) and 2.7b (Opposite) Kindergarten word walls for writing

writing errors that have little to do with a lack of word feature mastery and everything to do with repeatedly practicing an incorrect spelling. As an example, I offer *thay* for *they*. "Thay howl at the moon," "Thay are my best friends," "I don't know why thay do that." If I had a nickel for every sentence I've read in the last twenty-five years that contained a misspelled *they*, I'd have enough money to buy a summer home in the Hamptons! Other chronic misspellings I've encountered include *are* for *our*, *your* for *you're*, *gril* for *girl*, *their* for *they're*, *wen* for *when*, *wuz* for *was*, *vary* for *very*, and *cos* or *becuz* for *because*.

Because practice makes permanent, it is difficult to stamp out these types of misspellings. The good news is that children can be taught to self-monitor and spell correctly, especially if we give them the tools to do it. But let me first discuss what *not* to give them.

I'm convinced we should not teach a one-time list comprised of twenty words that children are expected to correctly use while writing. Nor should we incorporate a few writing words such as *they*, *want*, and *does* into our regular weekly spelling lists. In the past, I've used both of these methods, and neither of them got my students to transfer correctly spelled words into their day-to-day writing.

I suggest you look at your students' writing over the course of a few weeks and note one to three words that each child chronically misspells. I'll say that again. Note only *one, two, or three words* that each child chronically misspells. It's

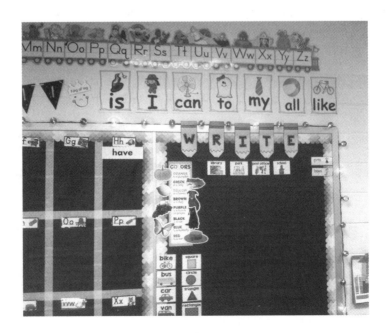

important that you focus on just a few words. Once you have one to three words, create a tool that writers can use to correct consistently misspelled writing words. These words can be specific to the class or specific to each child. By giving a tool that is easily accessible every time a child writes, you create the means to insist that your students spell certain words correctly each and every time.

What is this tool? It should be a simple device placed where students can easily find it. For words that most or many of your students misspell, the tool might be an anchor chart of two to three words. You can broadcast it on the Smartboard or hang the chart during writing time (Figure 2.8). Everyone should be able to see it. At the individual level, it might be an index card of one or two words taped to a desk or to the inside cover of a journal (Figure 2.9). Or it could be a short, ever-changing spelling list written on a special page in the same journal. If you determine that 60 percent of your class is misspelling *they*, then put the word *they* on the writing section of your word wall or add it to your writing-words anchor chart. But if only two children chronically misspell *they*, then that word

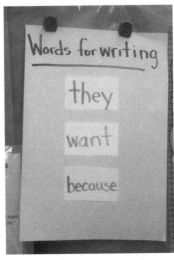

Figure 2.8 Classroom words-for-writing anchor chart

goes on the individual journal list or index card of those two children.

Sometimes chronically misspelled words arise from dialect. For example, many folks in western Pennsylvania turn long vowel sounds into short vowel

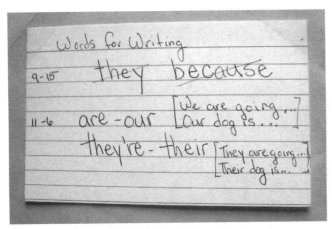

Figure 2.9 Individual words-for-writing index card

sounds, especially in words with the long *e* sound. Thus, *really* is pronounced *rilly*, and our beloved Steelers are called *Stillers*. Regardless of why students chronically misspell words, words that many of them frequently and consistently misspell when writing should go onto that anchor chart or index card.

Limiting an anchor chart to two to three words and an individual list to one or two words allows students to concentrate on and correct their most egregious spelling errors. It also allows you to manage assessment. If you pick too many words, students won't make progress in controlling their errors and you'll go crazy trying to keep track of any progress they are making. And you do want to track progress, because once you determine (through formative assessment) that the class or the individual has mastered a particular word, you'll want to take it off the anchor chart or list. If in the meantime another chronically misspelled word has popped up, then add that word to the chart or list. And if another word *hasn't* popped up, then take ten seconds and do a happy dance. Managing your classroom just got a little easier!

A Final Word on Assessment

I know that students and teachers are up to their ears in testing. In many districts, the instructional focus for the latter part of winter and the early part of spring is the high-stakes state test. This means that students in some schools spend almost a third of the school year preparing for and taking one test! It doesn't have to be this way, and in some states, districts and parents are pushing back.

But it's not just federal and state governments that force teachers into the rat race of testing. Sometimes districts are their own worst enemies. For example, districts mandate an avalanche of testing, including benchmark tests such as DIBELS and AIMSweb (three or more times a year), criterion-referenced tests such as the Developmental Reading Assessment (two or more times a year), and achievement or diagnostic tests such as STAR Literacy, Classroom Diagnostic Tools, the Iowa Test of Basic Skills, and the TerraNova. Yet in many instances these assessments don't need to be given as often as they are, or they provide redundant information. And some tests shouldn't be given at all because . . . wait for it . . . districts don't use the data! I know of schools that mandate fluency progress monitoring (via DIBELS) every three weeks, even for students who are well above fluency benchmarks. That's like ordering an adult to undergo blood testing every three weeks, each time reading the results and saying, "You are super-healthy."

Teachers also stoke the testing fires. Before my cooperating teacher and I changed our third-grade basal-based program, we sacrificed one 100-minute block of literacy instruction *every week* to give summative assessments in spelling, grammar, and the end of the week "unit" or "selection" test. Thus, every week our instructional time was cut by 20 percent. Even worse, we didn't really use our summative spelling test or selection test to plan our instruction. We just used it for a grade. Good grief!

So think formative, not summative. And remember that spelling is a means to an end, not an end in itself. Children do not spell words so that they can do well on a Friday spelling test. Children spell words so that they can read and write fluently. And as teachers, we shouldn't teach spelling to generate spelling scores. We should teach spelling to help students become better readers and writers so they can learn, expand their worldviews, and successfully share their thoughts, ideas, and dreams with others.

IF YOU HAVE ONLY TEN MINUTES

Meaningful formative assessment will take way more than ten minutes, but teachers have the ultimate busy schedule. If you have only ten minutes, here are concrete actions you can take.

- Give a spelling inventory at the beginning of the year.

- Give two struggling readers a phonics inventory. Compare the results of the phonics inventory to the results of the same students' spelling inventories.

- Analyze some independent writing samples three times a year to monitor growth.

- Give your class a weekly spelling test based on a list, but don't turn it into a time-consuming summative monster. Shoot for taking no more than ten minutes to give a spelling test.

EXPLORE CONNECTIONS

1. After giving a spelling inventory to your class, divide the inventory responses into three piles based on the number of misspelled words. Next, gather student writing samples. When you have ten or fifteen minutes of think time, sit down with the pile of spelling inventories that have the most misspelled words. Pick a specific student inventory and compare that inventory with the same student's writing sample. Do you see the same types of spelling errors in the writing sample that you see in the inventory? If not, what do you see? What does the comparison between these two assessments tell you?

2. Repeat the basic process outlined above, but this time use a spelling inventory, a phonics inventory, and an orally read passage on which you have marked student errors. Are miscalls on the oral reading passage the same as or different from the miscalls on the phonics inventory? How do the spelling inventory errors compare with the reading passage errors and the phonics inventory errors? Does it hold true that your student's spelling development is behind his or her current level of reading development?

CHAPTER 3

Focus Scope and Sequence

IN THIS CHAPTER

- We discuss ways to focus the scope of what you teach and slow down the rate at which you move through your spelling sequence. This is done to help students achieve spelling, reading, and writing mastery.

- We explore ways of creating word lists that support best-practice spelling instruction. Word list creation involves modifying established lists to create new ones that are rich and deep yet focused on just a few concepts.

Focusing and Slowing Your Scope and Sequence

Slow is not a bad thing, and neither is focused. Sure, *slowpoke* is an unflattering description, and *focused* can be synonymous with single-minded. But when we look at slow and focused through the lens of instruction, we understand that slowing down and focusing provide us with a chance to thoroughly teach material and give our students opportunities to master critical skills. Adopting a slower pace and a more targeted curriculum allows for richness and depth in lessons. And a slow and focused mind-set gives both teacher and students the opportunity to enjoy the learning process.

Here are some general guidelines for creating a spelling scope and sequence that covers less material and allows room for reteaching, which in turn helps more students become better readers and writers.

Teach Less to Teach More

When it comes to making changes in spelling instruction, a fine place to start is tightening up your spelling sequence. Some spelling sequences are simply too long, with too many discrete weekly lessons. The longer the sequence (twenty-five steps, twenty-nine steps, thirty-two steps), the more you are forced to move quickly to cover the material. My suggestion is to modify your sequence by strategically condensing its number of steps.

Figure 3.1 shows a second-grade sequence in its original form of twenty-seven weekly lessons and in its modified form of twenty-one lessons. My modifications included doubling up on vowel-consonant-*e* lessons (which allows me to teach comparing and contrasting of vowel sounds), taking out a lesson that is thoroughly covered in third grade (*oi/oy*), taking out a lesson that teaches an infrequent spelling pattern (*ar* as in *parable*), and combining *ch, tch,* and *ph* into one lesson. For another example of a pared-down sequence, look at

Grade 2 Original Sequence (27 Steps)	Grade 2 Revised Sequence (21 Steps)
short vowels	short vowels
/i/: i_e	/i/: i_e, /o/: o_e
/o/: o_e	
/u/: u_e	/u/: u_e, /a/: a_e
/a/: a_e	
/i/: igh, y, ie	/i/: igh, y, ie
/o/: oa, ow, oe	/o/: oa, ow, oe
/e/: ee, ea, y	/e/: ee, ea, y
ch, sh, th, wh	ch, sh, th, wh
ch, tch	ch, tch, ph
ph	
spr, str	spr, str
ar, or	ar, or
er, ir, ur	er, ir, ur
oo, ou, ui, ew, oe, ue	oo, ou, ui, ew, oe, ue
au (e.g., Paul), aw	au (e.g., Paul), aw
ow, ou	ow, ou
oi, oy	
schwa	
gn, kn, wr, mb	gn, kn, wr, mb
hard/soft c and g	hard/soft c and g
ge, dge, lge, nge, rge	ge, dge, lge, nge, rge
ar (e.g., parable)	
air, are	air, are
eer, ere, ear	eer, ere, ear
or, ore, oar	or, ore, oar
ire, ure	ire, ure

Figure 3.2 (Left) Revised spelling sequence

Figure 3.2 (Opposite) Final revised spelling sequence and scope

the nineteen-step first-grade lesson sequence in Appendix B.

Having fewer lessons gives you time to reteach concepts and patterns. When you have space in your sequence to accommodate reteaching, you won't need to push kids into a new concept before they have mastered the previous one.

After you've tightened the sequence, narrow the scope. Look over the spelling concepts and patterns you introduce each week and consider reducing the number you teach per lesson. If, for example, you see a lesson that teaches five or six patterns, identify the low-frequency spelling patterns and take them out. Figure 3.2 shows how I took the revised second-grade sequence and reduced the number of spelling patterns presented in eight of the remaining twenty-one lessons.

Grade 2 Original Sequence (27 Steps)	Grade 2 Revised Sequence (21 Steps)	Grade 2 Revised Sequence and Scope
short vowels	short vowels	short vowels
/i/: i_e	/i/: i_e, /o/: o_e	/i/: i_e, /o/: o_e
/o/: o_e		
/u/: u_e	/u/: u_e, /a/: a_e	/u/: u_e, /a/: a_e
/a/: a_e		
/i/: igh, y, ie	/i/: igh, y, ie	/i/: igh, y
/o/: oa, ow, oe	/o/: oa, ow, oe	/o/: oa, ow
/e/: ee, ea, y	/e/: ee, ea, y	/e/: ee, ea, y
ch, sh, th, wh	ch, sh, th, wh	sh, th, wh
ch, tch	ch, tch, ph	ch, tch, ph
ph		
spr, str	spr, str	spr, str
ar, or	ar, or	ar, or
er, ir, ur	er, ir, ur	er, ir, ur
oo, ou, ui, ew, oe, ue	oo, ou, ui, ew, oe, ue	oo, ui, ew
au (e.g., Paul), aw	au (e.g., Paul), aw	au (e.g., Paul), aw
ow, ou	ow, ou	ow, ou
oi, oy		
schwa		
gn, kn, wr, mb	gn, kn, wr, mb	kn, wr, mb
hard/soft c and g	hard/soft c and g	hard/soft c and g
ge, dge, lge, nge, rge	ge, dge, lge, nge, rge	ge, dge
ar (e.g., parable)		
air, are	air, are	air, are
eer, ere, ear	eer, ere, ear	eer, ear
or, ore, oar	or, ore, oar	or, ore
ire, ure	ire, ure	ire, ure

I believe in pruning low-frequency spelling patterns for two crucial reasons. First, there is much to teach and little time in which to teach it. Why spend valuable time teaching patterns that students don't often encounter? Take a look at Figure 3.3 and you'll see that many vowel patterns occur infrequently. In fact, the *ie* spelling of the long *i* vowel sound and the *oar* spelling of the *or* vowel sound occur so infrequently that they don't even appear on the chart! Why teach the *oar* spelling of the *or* vowel sound when a second grader might encounter it in *oar* and *board,* and that's about it? And why teach the *ie* pattern when *pie* is the only word a second grader might write? Teach the correct spelling of these words if and when you need to, not as part of your regular spelling instruction.

Specific vowel sounds in the majority of words (approximately 75 percent or more) are spelled using only two or three specific graphemes.

Phoneme	Grapheme (word example)	% of Use*	Phoneme	Grapheme (word example)	% of Use*
/i/	i (sit) i_e (give) y (gym)	92 6 2	/u/	u (cup) o (cover)	86 8
/e/	e (bed) ea (breath)	91 4	/oi/	oi (oil) oy (boy)	62 32
/a/	a (cat) a_e (have)	97 3	/er/	(her) or (odor) ar (cellar)	77 12 8
/a/	a (baby) a_e (make) ai (rain) ay (play)	45 35 9 6	/ou/	ou (out) ow (cow) ou_e (house)	56 29 13
/e/	y (happy) e (me) ee (see) ea (eat)	41 40 6 6	/u/	oo (moon) u (truth) o (who) u_e (tube) ou (through)	38 21 8 7.5 6.4
/i/	i_e (time) i (pi) y (cry) igh (right)	37 37 14 6	/ar/	ar (cart) are (are) ear (heart)	89 5 3
/o/	o (fox) a (swap)	94 5	/or/	or (sport) ore (core)	96 3

(Hanna, Hanna, Hodges, and Rudorf 1966; Fry 2004)
*Not all graphemes are included; thus, totals do not equal 100 percent.

Note: The table and the notes above are from *LETRS Module 3: Spellography for Teachers: How English Spelling Works*, 2nd ed., p. 32, by L. C. Moats. 2005. Boston, MA: Sopris West. Copyright © 2005 by Sopris West Educational Service.

Figure 3.3 Frequency of graphemes for English vowel phonemes

Second, presenting fewer unknowns in any given lesson is best instructional practice. As teachers, we learn to analyze a complex task to fully understand it and present it effectively. If we present too many steps at once, students fail to learn, become frustrated, and may give up. Lessening the cognitive load by presenting fewer spelling concepts in each lesson allows us to build success for students, thereby strengthening the cycle of success, motivation, and learning.

Align Your Phonics and Spelling Scope and Sequence

If you have a basal program, you have a spelling scope and sequence. You also have a phonics scope and sequence. Because encoding and decoding are two sides of the same coin (the alphabetic principle), there really should be no mismatch between the scope and sequence of the two. Rather, phonics and spelling should be marching down the road arm in arm, in lockstep.

The bad news is that the older your reading series is, the more likely it is that the scope and sequence of its phonics and spelling are not aligned. The good news is that many of the newer basal reading series are doing a much better job of aligning the two. Still, at some point you should determine this for yourself by sitting down and carefully comparing the scopes and sequences. If they don't match, I suggest you reconfigure them so that they do. Instruction is more powerful when teachers teach the same sequence of spelling and phonics concepts and teach children explicitly that spelling is for reading.

If you teach spelling and phonics without a scope and sequence, I recommend that you find one or, if you have the experience and the knowledge to do so, create one. All teachers can benefit from an organizational tool like a scope and sequence. It allows you to track your instruction, follow the progress of your students along a continuum of development, and modify your instruction based on that progress. Not having a scope and sequence can seriously impede the progress of your students in reading, especially for those who struggle. So make sure you have a spelling scope and sequence, which you can get by

- reconfiguring one from an older reading series, as I did in Figures 3.1 and 3.2;
- borrowing one from a recently published reading series;
- creating one using the developmental continuum and the spelling features outlined in this book's development chart (refer to Figure 1.3);
- creating one using the developmental continuum and the spelling

features from a detailed spelling inventory (such as one given in Appendix A of this book); or

- using the scope and sequence of syllable types, as outlined in an encoding-decoding program such as Wilson Reading.

Further Suggestions for Scope and Sequence

Regardless of where your scope and sequence comes from, here are some additional suggestions on how to think about teaching it.

- **Commit to teaching short vowel sounds to mastery.**

When students fail to master short vowel sounds and their spellings but are still pushed into long vowel sounds and their spellings (for example, in VC*e* words or words with vowel teams), they quickly become confused. This confusion leads to guessing about the spelling of vowel sounds. Researchers such as Invernizzi and Hayes (2004) suggest that students must master short vowel patterns (or closed syllables) before they can successfully navigate long vowel patterns. Other researchers explicitly say, "[I]t is the teacher's responsibility to continue to work on a phonics skill, using differentiated small-group instruction until data suggest that students are ready to move on" (Dewitz and Jones 2013, 396). In other words, take your time and teach short vowels, with the intention of giving kids a solid foundation.

The human brain is a pattern-loving machine: it looks for patterns in faces, in the environment, in historical events, and in the behavior of others. Patterns, or systematic and predictable relationships, are how we make sense of the world. Thus, patterns in words, or the stable relationship between sounds and letters (aka phonics), are how children make sense of reading and writing. Short vowel patterns such as *at, ock, ip, ish, ump* are a young child's first encounter with word predictability (beyond simple one-to-one sound-letter relationships), and if they don't master these relationships and understand them as predictable, then the decoding and encoding ground they stand on isn't very firm. A flimsy foundation leads to erroneous learning later on, so that by the third grade, a child may be sinking in a quicksand of confused phonics. He doesn't know if *tine* says *tine* or *tin* or if *plan* says *plane* or *plan*. Helping a young student build mastery over spelling short vowel patterns before rushing into long vowel patterns, then, can provide firm, strong ground on which students can build a beautiful house of effective reading and writing.

Once you have made a commitment to not automatically moving through a spelling sequence, you have the opportunity to provide instruction that allows students to master skills. This instruction may encompass reteaching a unit, differentiating word lists for different learners, using activities that teach children how spelling works, and increasing the amount of direct and explicit instruction you give to certain children.

- **Spend more time teaching vowel sounds and patterns and less time teaching consonant sounds and patterns.**

This idea goes hand in hand with teaching short vowel sounds to mastery. For many children, it is much harder to hear vowel sounds and to master the many vowel spellings that pair with them than it is to hear and spell consonant combinations. So put more time into vowels than into consonants.

Some spelling programs devote too much time to the teaching of consonant combinations, such as *bl, cl, fl, st, str, sp, spl,* and *spr.* If early on you teach your students how to segment and blend words and syllables, and to stretch out words and syllables so they can hear individual sounds, then you don't need to spend as much time on these consonant combinations. If you are in need of activities for teaching segmenting and blending, Chapter 6 describes some effective ones that are easy for you to implement and fun for kids to do.

- **Reorganize your scope and sequence into seven syllable types.**

The letter combinations of words can be categorized and then taught in any number of ways: short vowels, long vowels, other vowels, altered vowels, easy affixes, harder affixes, *l*-controlled, *r*-controlled, inflected endings, unaccented final syllables, bases, roots, oddities . . . I could go on. I suggest you make it easy on your students and easy on yourself by thinking in terms of seven basic syllable types: closed, open, vowel-consonant-*e*, vowel-team, *r*-controlled, consonant–*le* (sometimes called final stable), and "leftovers."

Teaching seven syllable types (Figure 3.4) provides students with a strategy that makes both encoding and decoding easier, especially when they start to tackle the reading and spelling of multisyllabic words. But I'm getting ahead of myself. We'll fully explore the seven syllable types, and strategies for teaching them, in Chapter 5.

Syllable Type	Examples
Closed	at, shrink, moss, puppet, fantastic
Open	go, she, flu, lady, baby, hero, potato
Vowel-consonant-*e*	ate, hike, Rome, lifetime, valentine
Vowel team	eat, green, throat, cloud, guardrail, headway
R-controlled	or, horn, star, germ, third, farmer, surgery
Consonant-*le*	able, bugle, rifle, puzzle, ripple, people
Leftovers	nature, natural, nation, explosion

Figure 3.4 The seven basic syllable types

- **Think in terms of a few broad principles.**

Many spelling rules have so many variations and exceptions that they don't help children understand how words work. For example, the rule "*I* before *E* except after *C*" applies only to words in which the *ie* combination functions as a vowel digraph that clearly says *e*, as in *piece, chief, yield, deceit, ceiling,* and *receive.* It doesn't work for words in which the digraph says *a,* as in *weigh, eight, beige,* and *vein,* or in words such as *foreign, forfeit, heifer,* and *height.* Nor does it apply to words in which an adjacent *i* and *e* aren't a digraph, such as in *deity* and *science* and their various derivations (*deify, deification, prescience, scientific,* and so on). Finally, even when a vowel digraph makes the *e* sound, there are exceptions to "*I* before *E.*" Here I am thinking of *seize, weird, either, neither, protein,* and *caffeine,* among others. In the end, "*I* before *E*" has so many variations and exceptions that as a rule it is rendered mostly useless.

If you want to teach children how to determine if they should put the *e* first or the *i* first, I'd suggest you teach a principle rather than a rule. For example, teach that certain vowel-team patterns are highly stable in their pronunciation (such as *eigh, ief, ield*). Put into more child-friendly language, "The *eigh* pattern almost always says *AY,* and the *ief* pattern almost always says *EEF*" (Figure 3.5). Teach your students these patterns (not rules) and then give them many opportunities to spell, write, and read the patterns in many different words. The more they spell, read, and write words with patterns, the more they will enter these words into the dictionaries in their brains.

Another spelling rule that teachers often give is "When two vowels go walking, the first one does the talking." Like "*I* before *E* except after *C,*" the "two vowels go walking" rule does little to help students develop an understanding of spelling patterns within words. How does it help them read or spell the words *great, vein, their, you, piece, height, spoon, spread, spoil, noun, heard,* and *double*?

EIGH says *a*. *a* is often spelled *eigh*.	IEF says *eef*. *eef* is often spelled *ief*.	IELD says *eeld*. *eeld* is often spelled *ield*.	CEI says *see*. *see* is often spelled *cei*.
weigh	brief	field	ceiling
sleigh	debrief	outfield	receive
inveigh	chief	fieldstone	deceive
eight	chieftain	yield	conceive
weight	thief	wield	perceive
weighty	fief	shield	misperceive
freight	fiefdom	Garfield	conceit
eighteen	grief	windshield	conceited
neigh	lief*	unwieldy	deceit
neighbor	belief		deceitful
neighborhood	disbelief		receipt
	*archaic		

Figure 3.5 Vowel-team patterns with stable pronunciations

A much more useful principle is this: a sound's position often determines its spelling. Because there are often many spellings for one vowel sound, vowel spellings can seem horribly complicated. But when you teach students to be guided by sound position, vowel spellings become more predictable. For example, the *ou* sound can be spelled *ou* or *ow*. Before children have committed whole words like *cloud, clown, outer,* and *flower* to the dictionaries in their brains, they need a way to decide how to spell the *ou* sound. Is it *clowd* or *cloud*?

We can help students figure out which spelling to use by teaching them to think about where they hear the sound in a word. In this instance, you might tell your students that if the *ou* sound is heard at the beginning of a word, spell it *ou*. Then give examples (*ouch, out,* and *ounce*). If the *ou* sound is heard at the end of a word or syllable, use *ow* (as in *cow, eyebrow,* and *flower*). And if *ou* is in the middle of a word or syllable, use *ou* (as in *mouse, loud,* and *grouch*). Finally, teach them an exception: if you hear *ou* in the middle of a one-syllable word and the vowel sound is followed by an *n* or *l* sound, then spell it *ow* (as in *brown, gown, howl,* and *growl*).

Other vowel spellings that can be determined by sound position include *oi* and *oy*, as well as *ai* and *ay*. Using the position of a sound in a word also works for consonant spellings. Thus, when you hear the *f, l,* or *s* sound after a short vowel sound in a one-syllable word, you double the *f, l,* or *s* (as in *fluff, bill,* and *glass*).

The main point: principles are easier to remember and more broadly applicable than dozens of individual rules.

Guidelines for Creating a Master Spelling List

Now that we have discussed a focused scope and sequence, let's talk about creating an effective spelling list that takes the form of what I call a master list. An effective master list is a nuanced thing. The best ones are developmentally appropriate, not too broad in the concepts they teach, varied in their levels of word difficulty, designed for differentiation, inclusive of words often used in writing, and flexible enough to be used with a variety of instructional activities. Creating such a list takes a bit of practice, but the more you practice, the better you get. To start, here are four guidelines for creating an effective master list for every spelling lesson:

1. For children in the early and early middle stages of spelling development, keep your list focused on only one or two concepts (sound-letter relationships, spelling patterns, or spelling conventions). For children in the more advanced stages of development, keep your list to three or four concepts (such as patterns, Latin/Greek roots, affixes, and conventions).

2. When choosing words, try to strike a balance between words that teach the spelling concepts you want to teach (sound, pattern, meaning, convention) and words that have high utility for students when they write. For example, if you are teaching the *i*-consonant-*e* pattern to second graders, you will pick words such as *ice, mile,* and *inside,* rather than *dice, fife,* and *incite.* And if you are teaching words that use closed and open syllables to third graders, you want to include words such as *respect, began,* and *finish,* rather than *virus, goblet,* and *enlist.*

3. Construct a master list (for yourself) that is at *least* thirty to thirty-five words long, with every word focused on the two to four spelling ideas you want to teach. From this list, pull ten to twenty words, depending upon the age of your students, to give as a pre-test.

4. After giving a pre-test, construct a shorter weekly word list for students, perhaps fifteen words long for older students and ten words or fewer for younger ones. And consider differentiating to create a number of shorter student lists. This will allow you to teach to a variety of achievement levels, varying word length or word meaning but staying within the parameters of Guideline 1.

There you have it: two to four spelling ideas taught per list, words appropriate for spelling and writing (as much as possible), a long word list for yourself, and a short weekly list or lists for your students. Before we move on, let's explore these ideas in a bit more depth.

Focus on Two to Four Spelling Ideas

When lists are focused, teachers have a better understanding of what exactly they are teaching. They are also better able to assess whether students have truly mastered a sound-letter combination, pattern, suffix, root word, and so on. Meanwhile, students have a better chance of mastering whatever is being presented.

You will have more success teaching English language learners and struggling readers when your word list for every lesson is narrow and deep. Imagine each week's spelling word list as the root system of a tree. You don't want it to be a dispersed web of many thin roots, made up of five, six, or seven spelling patterns and concepts, each represented by one, two, or three words. If you present too many concepts with too few examples, your lesson isn't anchored. If your lesson isn't anchored, your learners won't learn deeply; they'll just memorize now and forget later on. But if your list consists of two to four main roots, and if each root has a great many words branching from it, your students will have the chance to grow deep spelling roots of their own, roots that will anchor and sustain them throughout their independent reading and writing.

One last thing about two to four concepts: my classroom teaching has run the gamut from a self-contained special education classroom to cotaught inclusion classrooms with a wide spectrum of student ability and achievement (including students who are gifted). But my main educational focus has always been the struggling reader. Thus, my longtime motto has been "Plan for the struggling students and differentiate to reach the others." I believe that planning for fewer spelling patterns and concepts in each lesson and then differentiating by creating more challenging words *with the same patterns and concepts* lets you reach students in any number of stages of spelling development, from the early to the advanced.

Balance Spelling Concepts and Writing Words

When constructing your master list, think about the words children use in writing. A helpful resource for aligning spelling concepts with often-used writing words is *The Basic Spelling Vocabulary List* (Graham, Harris, and Loynachan 1993). According to the authors, the spelling vocabulary list they present contains "850 words that account for 80 percent of the words children use in their writing—the ones they need to be able to spell correctly" (363).

Another source of spelling lists that correlate with writing words is the Spelling Connections program by Zaner-Bloser. It is a large grade-by-grade program, however, and districts, not teachers, typically purchase it, so you might not have easy access to its lists of spelling words. But if you know someone who has a Spelling Connections teacher's manual for your grade level, I encourage you to look at its scope and sequence and its lists. Typically they are differentiated, lengthy, and varied, and the words contained in the weekly lists both demonstrate the spelling concept and are useful to students for their writing.

Also, use your teacher sense. As we teach within our grades, and as our students write, we increasingly gain a sense of what topics our students are writing about and what words they need to convey information on these topics. It pays to keep a large note card or small notebook (label it *Words for Writing*) in which you jot down words students use in their writing or words that occur to you as you think about upcoming lessons. When it comes time to create a master list for any given spelling lesson, scan through the words in your *Words for Writing* and see if any of them work with the spelling concept you want to teach. Thinking back to Chapter 2 and the third-grade boy who wrote about robots in Figure 2.5 (robots being a topic that was part of a third-grade science unit as well as a guided reading selection), I would have loved to have worked the writing words *robots*, *collect*, *volcano*, and *direct* into a master spelling list for a lesson on multisyllabic words spelled with open and closed syllables.

Construct a Long Master List for Yourself and Shorter Lists for Students

To use a variety of spelling activities in your classroom, and to teach students *how* to spell (as opposed to *what* to spell), you need a large number of words at your disposal. Pulling in a mixture of words from a variety of sources gives you real options for instruction. A lengthy master word list allows you to present multiple examples of a specific pattern, affix, or root, allows you to use different words in different activities, and helps you more easily differentiate for two or even three different groups of children (who are at different points on the developmental spelling continuum). Finally, a lengthy master list enables you to reteach lessons for a second or even a third week in a row without presenting the same words over and over again.

I'll end this section with a quote from renowned spelling researcher Dr. Richard Gentry, author of the Spelling Connections program. Concerning poor spelling instruction and the use of poorly constructed word lists, Gentry says, "Practices that lead to problems include no individualization, badly designed exercises, words irrelevant to writing, developmentally inappropriate words, too many worksheets, and testing words without teaching spelling" (2016a, Z21). But if you keep in mind the ideas presented in this book, your spelling practices won't have these problems. Construct your lists using the above guidelines and they will be focused on a few key spelling concepts, inclusive of writing words, useful for nonworksheet activities that teach children how to spell, and long enough to allow for individualization and reteaching. And you'll be well on your way to truly teaching spelling and giving your students a deeper understanding of words.

In the next chapter, we'll talk more about building a long word list. Right now, however, let's make sure we have a focused one.

Begin to Create a Focused Master Word List

In this section, we begin to create two master spelling lists. In the end they will look very similar. But here at the beginning, the two lists will look very different. This is because they begin in two very different types of classrooms. The first list is in the style of a basal spelling list. It will serve as an example for anyone using a basal program. The second list is in the style of a *Recipe for Reading* (Bloom and Traub 2000) list or a *Words Their Way* (Bear et al. 2012) word sort. This list is an example for anyone teaching in a balanced literacy or reading/writing workshop program who still needs a list, or who has a list that just isn't working.

Both example lists teach vowel-team patterns that make the long *u* sound. And both come from either a fourth-grade scope and sequence or a word list that can be used with fourth-grade children.

List Created from a Basal Program

The spelling list in Figure 3.6 is based on a list from a traditional fourth-grade basal program. If you use a major published program, such as Macmillan/McGraw-Hill's Treasures, Scott Foresman's Reading Street, or Harcourt's Storytown, then this list will seem familiar. Although not pulled from an actual program, it is similar to a list you can find in most fourth-grade basal program teacher's manuals. The asterisks next to some words signify challenge words.

flute	cruise	bamboo*
brood	usual	aluminum*
tooth	fuel	valuable*
chew	pupil	introduce*
juice	produce	communicate*
huge	groove	
scooter	confuse	
truth	humid	
bruise	ruby	
nephew	afternoon	

Figure 3.6 Word list based on a fourth-grade basal program list

Are there positives to this list? You bet.

- Its words vary in their number of syllables and in their vocabulary level.

- Words such as *usual, excuse, influence, accumulate,* and *confuse* have academic utility.

- A number of words would be useful to children when writing. For example, *usual, huge, juice,* and *afternoon* are all words students might use in a piece of prompt-based or self-selected topic writing.

Although this spelling list has positives, it also has negatives, and some of the negatives are profound. First and foremost, there are too many patterns for the target vowel sound (long *u*) and not enough examples of words that use each pattern. In other words, this list is too wide and too thin. Some spelling patterns, such *ew* and *ue*, are seen in only one or two words.

In addition, a teacher's manual might say this list presents five ways to spell the long *u* sound: *u*-consonant-*e*, *ui*, *u*, *ew*, and *oo*. But I'd say there are more. Why? This list contains a number of "oddball" words, words that don't exactly fit the five main spelling patterns. Take, for example, *fuel*, with its spelling of *ue*. Not only is the pattern presented in just one word, but the pure *u* sound is hard to hear. Another oddball word is *groove*, which is spelled with the *oo* vowel-team pattern (as in *brood* and *scooter*) but looks like a vowel-consonant-*e* word. If we want to explain how the word *groove* works, we need to teach the following spelling principle: because words in English typically don't end in *u* or *v*, spellers must add a silent *e* (marker) at the end. Think of *give, live, have, true, glue,* and *blue.*

One of my biggest beefs with spelling lists from published literacy programs is that they present five, six, and sometimes seven new things. Many lessons give too many patterns and concepts, making it difficult for a teacher to plan word study activities and give instruction on how spelling works. What's worse, lessons that present too much new information encourage a memorize-and-move-on style of teaching.

To make a basal list like this one better, let's agree to whittle down the number of patterns so we can teach the remaining ones more thoroughly. For our new list, we'll choose just two or three spelling patterns, such as the vowel-consonant-*e* and open syllables, or the *ui, ew,* and *oo* patterns. The point is to think about the basic spelling development level of the majority of your students, then focus your spelling list on only two to four sounds, patterns, affixes, or conventions of spelling. If the majority of your students are in the earlier stages of development, or if many of them are struggling readers and writers, limit your list to two spelling concepts. If you have many students who are in the middle or later stages of spelling development, or if you think the majority of your students can handle more than two concepts on a list, then go ahead and give them three or four to chew on. But I firmly believe that putting five or more patterns or concepts into one lesson is asking for trouble.

Figure 3.7 shows a revised, focused version of the spelling list of Figure 3.6. The revised list presents just three spelling patterns (*u*-consonant-*e, ui,* and *ew*) and sets the stage for a long *u* sound master list that is focused and deep.

huge	chew	juice
produce	nephew	cruise
confuse		bruise

Figure 3.7 Focused fourth-grade list (beginning of a master list)

Now we have eight tightly focused spelling words. If we think that *huge, confuse, chew,* and *produce* are words that students will use in writing, then this list adheres to two of the four general guidelines: it focuses on two to four concepts, and it contains some high-utility writing words. So much for the good news. The bad news is that the list lacks length and variety. If you're thinking, *Yikes! A master list of only eight words?* I understand. But don't worry. In the next chapter, we will add words to each pattern category to create a long master list flexible enough to be used for all types of instructional activities and for any number of differentiated student lists.

List Created in a Balanced Literacy or Workshop Classroom

In the last year and a half, I've had more than a few teachers approach me after one of my spelling presentations and say, "Our school has just gotten rid of our basal program and moved to a balanced literacy program. But we don't have anything to replace our spelling program! Do you think we should teach using spelling lists? If so, where do we get them?"

Our second example list presents ideas for anyone who is teaching in a balanced literacy classroom or using a workshop model and is in need of a spelling list. Like the basal list, this list addresses patterns that make the long *u* sound, and it can be used with fourth-grade students. It can also be used in other grades, depending upon the readiness of your students.

If you are in the predicament of not having a list, never fear. Words for spelling lists can be gathered from any number of places. Wilson Language products are full of words that are suitable for teaching spelling patterns, inflectional endings, suffixes, and the like. The word sorts in the back of *Words Their Way* are well written and very useful. Other programs include Spelling Connections from Zaner-Bloser, Signs for Sounds™ from Read Naturally, and Recipe for Reading® from EPS, among others. Just remember that before picking words for a list, you'll need to have a scope and sequence in place, as we discussed earlier in this chapter.

The following list is constructed from a word sort similar to one that you would find in a book such as *Words Their Way*. Rather than spelling lists, this type of program gives word sorts as the starting point for spelling instruction. But in Figure 3.8 I have taken a word sort and presented it as a fourth-grade spelling list.

rude	new	juice	*
prune	few	bruise	fuel
flute	chew	cruise	cruel
rule	grew	fruit	gruel
tune	knew	suit	build
brute	stew		guilt
use	threw		

Figure 3.8 Word list based on a stand-alone program's word sort

This list begins with more positives than the previously mentioned basal-based list:

- The words fall into a limited, focused number of pattern categories: *ui, ew,* and *u-consonant-e*.

- There are five or more words given in each of the three categories. Thus, this list has both focus and depth, which makes it more useful for high-quality spelling instruction.

- The list provides a limited number of noncategory words. These "oddballs" fall under the asterisk.

This list is focused, it contains a fair number of words, and it is laid out so that comparisons between words can be made easily. What more can be done? To get this list into a master list format appropriate for all learners, I suggest adding more complex words, which we will do in the next chapter. Additionally, I'd limit the number of oddball words to one pattern category, either *uel* or *uil*. If my classroom had children still struggling to hear and reproduce vowel sounds, I would pick the *uil* pattern, because its short *i* sound is easier to distinguish from the *oo* and *yoo* sound of *ew, ui,* and *u-consonant-e*. Furthermore, I would include only *build*, because *guilt* is a word students are less likely to use in writing and because *build* is a base word that can be transformed into *built, builds, rebuild, building,* and *Bob the Builder*. Of course, the choice is yours. *Guilt* might work well for the students you are teaching. There is no absolute wrong or right to the construction of a spelling list. In its focused form, the list shown in Figure 3.9 provides a great start to a master list.

use	new	juice	*
rude	few	bruise	build
tune	chew	cruise	
flute	grew	fruit	
brute	knew	suit	
prune	stew		
rule	threw		

Figure 3.9 Word list based on a stand-alone program's word sort

If you'd like to see additional examples of focused lists for both basal-based programs with traditional lists and balanced literacy programs in need of a list, please look at Appendix C, where you will find additional examples.

What's Next?

Okay! You have successfully moved from understanding to taking action. Specifically, you have instituted specific types of assessment, narrowed and slowed your instruction to promote mastery learning, and begun to create a flexible and effective master word list. You are well on the way to transforming your philosophy of spelling instruction. In the next chapter, we'll take another step, which is to populate a strong but sparse word list with more words, thereby making it a deep, varied, and very useful master list. Then we will discuss how to create shorter differentiated lists from the master.

IF YOU HAVE ONLY TEN MINUTES

You can begin to take action on your instruction and your lists, even if you have only ten minutes.

- If you are a first- or second-grade teacher using a basal reading program, take a look at your grade-level scope and sequence. Find a consonant-based lesson (or two) that can be combined with another or taken out completely. Then insert a reminder to "reteach short vowels" in the newly found space or spaces.

- If you are a teacher of third graders, fourth graders, or fifth graders, take a look at the spelling list you are going to teach next week. Count up the number of unique spelling concepts that are being taught in one lesson. For example, is your lesson teaching *j* as in *giant, junior,* and *budge, ks* as in *excuse, sk* as in *schedule,* and *s* as in *science* and *justice*? If so, you are exposing your students to seven spelling patterns and concepts in one lesson! Think about which four you might want to concentrate on.

EXPLORE CONNECTIONS

1. What words on a spelling list might be useful to students when they write? Do you think there are words on your spelling list that (1) aren't a good match for the pattern being taught and (2) probably aren't useful to student writers in your classroom?

2. What did you learn in Chapter 1 that applies to this chapter?

3. How do encoding and decoding relate to each other? Do you believe focused spelling lists are important tools for getting children to the point of reading fluency? If so, why? If not, why not?

CHAPTER 4

Bring More Words

Ecosystems and Brain Dictionaries

Spelling instruction functions like an ecosystem, its components working together to create a functioning structure greater than the sum of its parts. The components are intimately linked to one another. Remove one and the system begins to fail, or stops working all together.

A spelling ecosystem won't work without a focused scope and sequence, carefully constructed word lists, and activities that engage and instruct. To understand why all three are needed, we must remember how effective spelling instruction works on the brain. Spelling instruction activates the brain circuitry that stores, in the orthographic processing area, the following: letters, letter pairs, patterns, morphemes (meaning "chunks"), and complete words. The order in which these are stored mirrors a child's reading, writing, and spelling development: words are built up from separate stored sound-letter matches, then chunks, and later whole words. Instruction combined with word lists is the means for moving words into storage.

Note that the ultimate goal of spelling instruction is the storage of whole words. Whole-word storage (proceeded by the storage of letters and sounds and then word parts) is critical for fluent reading, a process that effortlessly combines the matching of words that a reader sees with word meanings and word spellings stored in the brain. Because we know that fluent reading is dependent upon the instant recognition of *entire words*, an essential goal of spelling instruction is to build the repository of word spellings known as the "dictionary in the brain." A master list, focused on a few spelling concepts yet fat with words of various complexities and meaning, is a tool we use to build children's brain dictionaries. But the list of words is also the thing we want to store. Oddly, spelling words are both the content we deliver and one of the tools for delivering that content.

It's important to note, too, that spelling and vocabulary are intertwined. If we can deeply teach students the *meaning* of their spelling words, then we are building their vocabulary even as we teach sound and pattern recognition. In *Super Core* (Weakland 2014), I commented on the number of repetitions necessary for a student to learn and use a new vocabulary word. The number of necessary exposures varies according to the abilities of each student, and estimates in the literature vary from six to twenty exposures, but one can safely say at least seven to ten repetitions are necessary for a typical child to master the meaning and usage of any given vocabulary word (Webb 2007). By providing focused yet rich and lengthy spelling word lists (and subsequent activities in which children see, say, and use those words), you build opportunities for students to gain vocabulary words that they can use for reading, writing, and speaking.

Finding Words for a Master List

To build a dictionary in each and every student's brain, we need to create a diverse and lengthy list and populate it with words—lots of them. Words, of course, are all around us. They're also etched on the pages of our very own brain dictionaries. But rather than randomly scanning the hillsides for words, or relying solely on pulling words from our sometimes tired brains, let's bring in words from a few select resources.

Online Resources

Rhymezone.com is a useful and fun site for exploring spelling patterns and finding words. Simply type in a word that contains your target spelling pattern and then hit Search. Because the site is rhyme specific, not rime specific, searches produce words with different spellings for the same-sounding end chunk. For example, my search for words rhyming with *grain* yielded 593 results, from one-syllable words and names such as *brain, lane, Wayne,* and *feign* to five-syllable phrases such as *capital of Spain* and *tympanic membrane*!

Wordfind.info site also has a search engine. Type in the word with which you want to rhyme and the site brings up lists of words of varying lengths. I typed in the word *slow* and the search engine found dozens of words, ranging from three letters (*row, pro, foe*) to nineteen letters in length (*eenie-meenie-miney-mo*).

Finally, at morewords.com, you can search for words with any letter sequence found at the beginning of a word, within a word, or at the end of a word. I suggest you always search for a letter sequence at the end of a word. Otherwise, your search will bring hundreds of words, many of them without your target pattern. For example, a search for words containing *ite* brings up 1,700 words, including *credited* and *gaiter,* as well as *write* and *excite.*

For affixes and Greek and Latin roots, try learnthat.org. Learn That Word is a collaborative group of parents, educators, English language learners, and writers dedicated to building literacy, in their words, "one word at a time." The site provides lists of words, extensive at times, based on the most commonly used prefixes, suffixes, and Greek and Latin roots. For example, their word list for the Latin root *anim* (life, spirit) includes *animal, animate, inanimate, reanimate, animation, animus, animosity, equanimity, animatronic, magnanimous,* and many more.

Compound words are a way to ease younger students, as well as older struggling learners, into the spelling of longer multisyllable words. Often created from two one-syllable words, a compound word is easy to chunk because each syllable has meaning. Look for words that illustrate a clear-cut spelling pattern in each syllable. If you are lucky, you'll find words that exhibit the same syllable type twice in a row. For example *backpack, washtub,* and *lipstick* consist solely of closed syllables, and *grapevine, dateline,* and *faceplate* are made exclusively of vowel-consonant-*e* syllables. Compound words made from a two-syllable word plus a one-syllable word are the next step in complexity. *Fingerprint, waterfall,* and *superman* are impressively long words that are easy to break apart and spell.

A quaint resource for compound words is *English Compound Words and Phrases: A Reference List, with Statement of Principles and Rules* by F. Horace Teall (1892/2016). I've never seen a hard copy of the book, but I had fun perusing it when I accessed it through Google Books. The URL is rather lengthy, so head to https://books.google.com and type "Funk and Wagnalls, compound words" into the search bar. If you'd like to own the book, a Kindle edition is available, as is a reprint published by Forgotten Books. Written by Mr. Teall when he was department editor of the famous dictionary, the book contains thousands of compound words, as well as a fascinating chapter on the history of compound words in the English language (for all you word nerds).

Although many of the words in Teall's book are obscure, others are common enough and also fit useful spelling patterns, especially if you are teaching syllable types. A quick search through the *C* section yielded the following closed-syllable words: *cashbox, castoff, catnip, checklist,* and *chickenpox.* (Others, such as *chopblock, cottonmill, clockspring*, and *chippingchisel* were acceptable to Mr. Teall in 1892 but not to my 2017 Microsoft Word spell checker.) If you are interested in teaching closed-syllable "history words" such as *clockspring*, yet reticent to present them as true compound words, break them apart and present them as two-word phrases. But you'll need to give some explanation about the meaning: "Yes, children, once *all* clocks had hands on the outside, gears on the inside, and tiny springs that powered them!"

Rhyming Dictionaries

As a songwriter, I am occasionally in need of rhyming words, so I have a number of rhyming dictionaries sitting on my shelf. Arranged and cross-referenced by sound and pattern, rhyming dictionaries are perfect places for finding a plenitude of words, from *multitude* to *birds*, that fit the spelling patterns of your master word list. Most can be found in paperback and are thus inexpensive. My favorite is *The Scholastic Rhyming Dictionary* (Young 1994). I bought this one with Scholastic book order points and have used it for more than twenty years now. The other rhyming dictionaries sitting on my shelf are the *Capricorn Rhyming Dictionary* (Redfield 1986) and *Merriam-Webster's Pocket Rhyming Dictionary* (Merriam-Webster 2001).

Teacher Resource Lists and Books

For those of you teaching first and second grade, the commonly occurring phonograms are a great place to start brainstorming words. Especially helpful are Wylie and Durrell's thirty-seven high-frequency phonograms (Wylie and Durrell 1970), presented in alphabetical order in Figure 4.1. By adding consonants, blends, and digraphs to these simple word parts, it should be relatively easy for you to generate dozens of words for your students to spell and read. According to Wylie and Durrell, "Nearly 500 primary grade words are derived from these thirty-seven high-frequency phonograms" (788).

ack	ank	eat	ill	ock	ump
ail	ap	ell	in	oke	unk
ain	ash	est	ine	op	
ake	at	ice	ing	ore	
ale	ate	ick	ink	ot	
ame	aw	ide	ip	uck	
an	ay	ite	it	ug	

Based on Wylie, Richard E., and Durrell, Donald D. 1970. "Teaching Vowels Through Phonograms." *Elementary English* 47 (6): 787–788.

Figure 4.1 Thirty-seven high-frequency phonograms

Be sure not to fall into the trap of doing all the work yourself. Put your students to work! Students can use flip books, magnet tiles, and old-fashioned paper and pencil to generate real and make-believe words from common phonograms. Have a spelling list party, where students generate words that end up on your master list for next week's lessons. They'll be tickled when they find that one of their words has made it into a spelling activity, and even more pleased if the word makes it onto their take-home spelling list.

Moving from Wylie to Wiley (holy author anagrams, Batman!), Wiley Blevins is the creator of useful resources for spelling words, including the best-selling *Phonics from A to Z* (Blevins 2006), as well as *Teaching Phonics and Word Study in the Intermediate Grades: A Complete Sourcebook* (Blevins 2001). In his books, Blevins provides banks of words that can be easily transferred into your master word lists.

Finally, the Teacher's Book of Lists is a series of books that provide words for spelling, writing, vocabulary building, and more. Although I've never used these books, teachers I respect tell me they use them, so I feel safe in recommending them. Two books from the series useful for spelling are *The Spelling Teacher's Book of Lists* (Phenix 2008) and *The Vocabulary Teacher's Book of Lists* (Fry 2004).

Resources from Spelling and Reading Programs

If you want to organize your spelling instruction by syllable types (see Chapter 5 for more), then the two Wilson language dictation books (Wilson 1996) are a must. Each book presents hundreds of words organized by the traditional six syllable types. The books also present sentences for reading and for dictation, with each sentence constructed from decodable and encodable words based on specific syllable types.

Also, I've mentioned *Words Their Way* (Bear et al. 2012) numerous times, as well as *Recipe for Reading* (Bloom and Traub 2000). Both books contain word sorts and word lists, which you can use as foundations for the master spelling lists you are creating.

Expertise and Experience

Last but certainly not least, use your own knowledge of words to add words to your master lists. If you are a lover of words like I am, it may be a pleasure to sit down and generate a list of words that fit your target spelling pattern or patterns, like these, which end with a consonant-*le* and have doubled consonants at the syllable juncture: *paddle, piddle, fiddle, battle, rattle, jiggle, wiggle, stubble, apple, scrapple, Scrabble, dribble, babble, bubble, Barney Rubble, Edwin Hubble,* and I could go on!

Crafting Master Word Lists

Now that we know where to find words, let's bring some in and finalize the lists we started in Chapter 3. Remember: these two lists had very different beginnings, the first starting as a basal spelling list and the second beginning as a word sort, and therefore looked quite different from each other when we ended the last chapter. But by the time we are finished with them in this chapter, the two lists will look very much the same.

Master Word List Created from a Basal Reading Program List

Think back to the focused spelling list in Figure 3.7 at the end of Chapter 3, which presented three spelling patterns (*u*-consonant-*e*, *ui*, and *ew*) and eight words. To this strongly focused but short list, we can now add words from our resources, building the number of words in each pattern category and creating a master list that can provide words for a number of differentiated student lists and a variety of spelling activities.

The list in Figure 4.2 presents plenty of one- and two-syllable words in each of the three pattern categories, as well as some three- and four-syllable words made by adding prefixes and suffixes. The list also includes a few two-word phrases, such as *juice box* and *cruise ship*. Although they aren't compound words, I think these little phrases work well for three reasons: (1) they fit the patterns, (2) the phrases, especially *juice box*, will be familiar to kids, and (3) the second word in each phrase is a simple monosyllabic short vowel word that does not bring additional spelling concepts into the lesson. Besides, there is no rule that a spelling list must contain only single words.

huge	new	juice
cute	few	cruise
brute	dew	bruise
tune	brew	suit
June	chew	fruit
rude	drew	bruises
crude	knew	swimsuit
flute	stew	suitcase
produce	threw	fruitcake
confuse	cashew	cruise ship
conclude	curfew	juice box
intrude	renew	cruising
excuse	nephew	bruising
tuning	outgrew	suitable
confusing	renewing	unsuitable
excusing		
producing		
reproduce		

Figure 4.2 Fourth-grade master word list

By sticking to just three core spelling patterns but adding longer words with endings, prefixes, and suffixes, we have created a master list that can be used with two or even three different groups. Figure 4.3 illustrates this idea, using the words from the master list to create three lists for an imagined fourth-grade classroom. In this imagined classroom are twenty-four fourth graders who have just taken a Monday morning pre-test that assesses their knowledge of the week's spelling patterns. What we have learned from the pre-test is that the kids fall into roughly three groups of spelling knowledge.

Perhaps the first small group consists of six children who are really sailing along in spelling and reading. They have mastery of patterns within words and don't need any basic teaching on the core patterns. For these students we can offer a list tilted toward root words and affixes, with words such as *confuse, conclude, produce, reproduce, renew,* and *unsuitable.*

The second group might consist of ten students who are not yet in control of the "drop *e,* add *ing*" rule. For this group we might create a list heavy with words that take the *ing* inflectional ending. Thus, in addition to *brute, knew,* and *curfew,* their list of words might include *confusing, cruising,* and *bruising,* which are formed from *confuse, cruise,* and *bruise.*

The final group of six might be made up of children still firmly in the "patterns in words" stage. These children need additional practice on the three basic patterns. Their word list might include one-syllable words in each of the patterns, as well as a few compound words such as *suitcase* and *fruitcake.*

Small Group 1	Small Group 2	Small Group 3
For six advanced children	For ten children who need focus on the "drop *e,* add *ing*" rule	For six children still developing the use of patterns in words
produce	brute	huge
confuse	confuse	tune
conclude	excuse	June
intrude	knew	rude
excusing	curfew	crude
reproduce	threw	chew
cashew	suit	drew
curfew	cruise	knew
renew	bruise	threw
nephew	excusing	juice
cruise ship	confusing	bruise
bruising	leaving	fruit
unsuitable	cruising	suitcase
fruitcake	bruising	fruitcake

Figure 4.3 Three differentiated lists from a master word list

Balanced Literacy Classroom Master List

The second of the two lists presented at the end of Chapter 3 began as a word sort. Like the basal-based list, this word sort list presented three spelling patterns (*u*-consonant-*e*, *ui*, and *ew*) in nineteen words, plus the "rule breaker" *build*.

Even though this list is already a fairly long one, we can still add words, just like we did to the basal-based list. The result will be the same: a large number of words in each pattern category that can be used to create differentiated student lists and run any number of spelling activities.

use	new	juice	*
rude	few	cruise	build
mule	dew	bruise	building
fume	brew	suit	builder
dune	chew	fruit	rebuild
crude	knew	bruises	rebuilding
cute	drew	cruising	built
tune	stew	bruising	prebuilt
June	threw	swimsuit	
rude	cashew	suitcase	
flute	curfew	fruitcake	
confuse	renew	cruise ship	
conclude	nephew	juice box	
intrude	outgrew		
excuse	chewing		
tuning	renewing		
confusing			

Figure 4.4 Fourth-grade master word list

As you can see in Figures 4.2 and 4.4, two lists that looked quite different at the beginning now look much the same. Each list focuses on just three vowel-team spellings, each contains simple one-syllable words as well as more complex two- and three-syllable words, and each is rich in vocabulary words, as well as words that children can use when they write. One difference between the two is that the second list early on included the word *build* (a *ui* pattern "rule breaker") and now contains a number of variations on it, such as *builder, building, built,* and *prebuilt*.

If you think your students will benefit from exposure to *build* and its variations, then perhaps you'll find this list to be the more useful of the two.

Which Words Do You Choose?

When choosing words for your master list, it pays to strike a balance between words that teach the spelling concept you want to get across and words that have high utility for writing. You'll have to use your teaching expertise to figure out this balance. For example, *gainsayer* and *great* are two words I came across while thinking about a master list focusing on the vowel teams *ai* and *ay*. At first I thought the choice was obvious: *gainsayer* goes on the list, *great* does not. Eventually I came to the opposite conclusion, and here's why. The word *gainsayer* uses the target long *a* sound patterns (*ai* and *ay*) in one word. But although I have taught second-grade students who were, in fact, energetic little gainsayers, I know second graders would never use this word in their writing and would rarely encounter it while reading. I rarely write or read it! Besides, there are plenty of other *ai* and *ay* words I can choose for my list. On the other hand, the word *great* contains neither *ai* nor *ay*, and the *ea* vowel team rarely makes a long *a* sound, but it's a useful word for second-grade writers. I am going to put that word on my master list, but I'll present it as a "rule breaker."

How Many Words for Students?

You don't need to include more than fourteen or fifteen words on a student's take-home spelling list, fewer for the youngest students. You'll notice that the three differentiated fourth-grade student word lists in Figure 4.3 contain only fourteen words each.

Not only do you not need twenty or twenty-five words on a student word list (although you can include that many if you want to), but you don't need to test students on every word on their list. Eight or ten might be more than enough. But the words should be randomly pulled from your students' take-home lists on the day of the test. Otherwise, your students might not practice spelling all of their words!

Giving an end-of-the-week test doesn't need to be a lengthy affair that tests dozens of words and eats up thirty minutes of instructional time every Friday. If you gather assessment information (with a few jotted notes, perhaps, as in Figure 4.5) from short quizzes, word study activities, and observation during word study activities, then your end-of-the-week test won't be the only place from which you are pulling scores for a grade. So choose just enough words to gather formative assessment information, generate a grade if you need to, and give your students a sense of accomplishment.

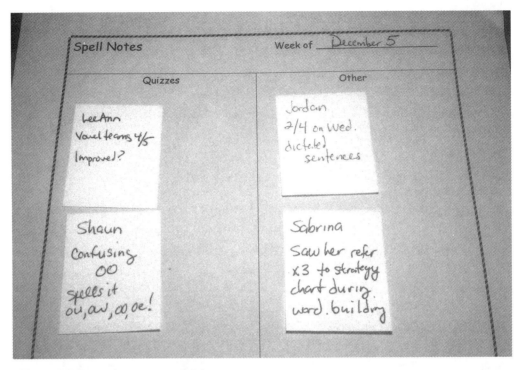

Figure 4.5 Formative assessment data

What's Next?

You are now well on the way toward transforming your philosophy of spelling instruction. Next comes a big step: transforming your day-to-day teaching. This step is large enough to require two chapters: one to address the teaching of strategies that students can use to become more accurate spellers, and one to address spelling activities that help students understand how words work while building that dictionary in their brains.

IF YOU HAVE ONLY TEN MINUTES

You can begin to take action on bringing words into a more effective spelling list, even if you have only ten minutes.

- Think about how you might divide your classroom into two groups based on your students' varying levels of spelling development. Make a list of the two groups.

- With two groups in mind, scan your current spelling list. Which words are more appropriate for Group 1? Which words are more appropriate for Group 2? Jot down two different lists.

- With these two spelling lists in hand, peruse one of the websites mentioned in this chapter. Find words appropriate for each of the two lists. Or brainstorm some words. Regardless of where they come from, add words to your two lists.

EXPLORE CONNECTIONS

1. What is the main purpose of a spelling list? How does it relate to reading? To writing?

2. How does this chapter connect with Chapter 3?

3. Regarding building master spelling lists, what are other possible sources of words? Are there resource books within your building? If there are, can teachers arrange to share them? What about vocabulary words from reading, social studies, or science? Can any of those words be added to a spelling master list?

CHAPTER 5

Teach Strategies

IN THIS CHAPTER

- We learn that spelling is something to be taught, not simply assigned.

- We examine a variety of strategies students can use when they are learning how to spell, not what to spell, and we consider ways of teaching these strategies to students.

- We understand that not all students employ the same strategy or strategies when spelling unknown words.

- We explore the seven syllable types and think about how this organizing principle can be used to organize and teach spelling words across grade levels.

Teaching, Not Assigning

Spelling is a subject to be taught, not assigned. Why? Effective spelling instruction helps children acquire critical reading skills, such as decoding, fluency, and vocabulary. It also enables children to become more fluent writers.

While talking with teachers in schools, on more than one occasion someone has said to me, "I don't teach spelling. I don't have the time! I give a list on Monday, a test on Friday, and that's it. My students have to be responsible for studying." Although I don't take issue with the need for students to be responsible, I do object to not teaching spelling, even as I understand why it happens. Burdened with loads of content to teach and not enough time, beleaguered teachers begin to sink under the weight of all there is to do. To stay afloat, they start heaving stuff off their sinking ship. Based on my experience, the pieces of instructional cargo most commonly tossed overboard are read-aloud, independent reading, student choice of writing topic, and deep, direct spelling instruction.

An emphasis on "memorize and move on" and "one size fits all" may be another reason some teachers fall into assigning spelling rather than teaching it. Nondifferentiated spelling programs with wide and unfocused lists make light of spelling-reading connections and underplay the importance of instruction, and their worksheets masquerade as meaningful opportunities to practice.

Fortunately, the burdens of too little time, too much to do, and "one size fits all" can be lightened without too much difficulty. Adopting a philosophy of differentiation and then giving a spelling inventory are good first steps toward solving the one-size-fits-all dilemma. Focusing a spelling word list on two to four concepts and then fleshing it out with dozens of words to accommodate a variety of spelling activities helps streamline the process. (Sound familiar?) Finally, having a collection of spelling strategies and a menu of teaching activities that support instructional efforts can help you find the right strategy for the right kid at the right time.

So let's move on to the teaching of spelling. In upcoming sections, we'll explore a number of strategies that students can use daily to encode and decode words in writing and reading. We'll also discuss an overarching instructional strategy to help categorize spelling instruction into syllable types, in order to rein in scope and sequence. And in the next chapter we'll look at spelling activities, some exploratory, some direct and explicit, and all stimulating, engaging, and useful for teaching sound, pattern, and meaning.

Teaching Students Strategies They Can Use

Just as it is useful to have strategies for driving—setting the cruise control to avoid inadvertently speeding on the highway, regularly checking your mirrors in heavy traffic, leaving a big city before rush hour begins—it is useful for students to have strategies for reading, writing, and spelling. Whether it's adjusting their reading rate, reading a piece of writing out loud to check for errors, or spelling unknown words by assigning letters to sounds, all children make use of strategies. To get to the point where they use strategies automatically, students must first practice them intentionally. Thus, they need for us to explicitly teach and model strategies, provide guidance as they use them, and step back and allow them to independently practice what they've learned.

Even before we teach strategies, however, we need to raise students' awareness that when they are spelling, it's a sure bet that they will occasionally, or even regularly, misspell words. Thus, we should tell our students, "All spellers make mistakes," and quickly follow that with "Spellers work to fix their mistakes." We want our students to know that when they don't know how to spell a word, they can use a strategy to ensure that it's spelled correctly.

Figure 5.1 shows a sample anchor chart of the spelling strategies described in the upcoming sections. As you read them and then teach some of them in your classroom, note how they relate to the stages of reading and spelling development, are useful in the development of reading and writing skills, and can be especially helpful to spellers who struggle.

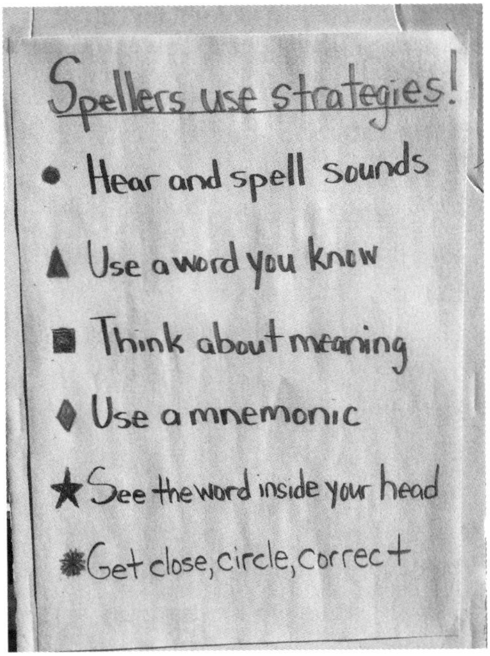

Figure 5.1 Spelling strategies anchor chart

Hear and Spell the Sounds: Stretch, Zap, Chin Drop

In the earliest stages of spelling, spellers hear a word aloud or in their heads (audiation) and then translate or encode the sounds into letters. To help your students notice the sounds in words (so they can assign letters to them), help them develop phonemic awareness. Phonemic awareness, a subset of phonological awareness, can be defined as the ability to hear, identify, and manipulate the phonemes (or sounds) of a language. For example, if English-speaking children are phonemically aware, they can understand that the word *slip* is made up of sounds, hear four separate sounds in the word, identify them as *s, l, i,* and *p,* and even, at a more advanced level, mentally leave off the first sound to make the word *lip,* or move the first sound to the last position, thereby making the word *lips.* All of this identification and manipulation occurs at the sound level, not the letter level.

Phonemic awareness is one step in the development of reading and spelling. A second step is sound-letter relationships, often called the alphabetic principle. This principle flows in two directions. To read the word *lap,* a kindergarten child must segment it into its component sounds—*l, a, p*—and then blend them together to make a word. To spell the word *lap,* the child segments the sounds and then assigns correct letters to each sound. At first, encoding and decoding a word may involve a series of matching one letter to one sound. The words *bat, flip,* and *slaps* lend themselves to this one-to-one sound and letter matching. Later, word chunks are recognized, such as the *ch* and *ur* chunks in the word *church* or the *th*, *ank*, and *ing* chunks in the word *thanking*. At this point spellers are entering the pattern recognition stage of spelling development. Still later, words are recognized in their entirety. Phonemic awareness and spelling development, then, are interrelated.

To best instruct on phonemic awareness, make your teaching explicit and direct, and provide lots of modeling. Speaking from personal experience, explicit phonemic awareness instruction not only works wonders for kindergartners, but can benefit struggling third and fourth graders as well. In all cases, it's best to keep in mind the zone of proximal development (giving kids what they need, wherever they happen to be developmentally) and gradual release of responsibility (having children eventually apply the strategy on their own).

While working in classrooms as a reading specialist, I learned a lot about teaching kids how to hear the sounds in words from an especially talented group of kindergarten teachers. All of them taught two specific techniques: stretching the word and zapping the sounds. Later, when children used these techniques to help them spell words, the techniques became spelling strategies.

Stretch the Word

To stretch a word, tell your students to imagine the word as a big rubber band. Grab hold of either end of the word (make two fists and hold them in front of you) and then slowly pull your hands away from each other, stretching the word out, holding out the vocalization of each phoneme as you stretch. Figure 5.2 shows second graders stretching the sounds of a word before spelling it. Some teachers teach this technique as "bubble gum words."

Keep in mind that some consonants can be held and stretched (*m, f, l, s, z*), whereas others cannot (*b, t, k, p*). So regardless of whether the word is a rubber band or a wad of gum, it's best to start with words that have consonants and vowels that can be "held," such as *f, l, m, s*, short *a*, and short *o*. Don't start with

Figure 5.2 Stretching a word to hear its sounds

words such as *bait* or *coin*. Start with words like *sat, moss,* and *flip,* which would be stretched as *sss-aaa-t, mmm-ooo-ssss,* and *fff-lll-iii-p*.

After the rubber band is stretched as far as it can go and all of the phonemes have been drawn out, snap the band back together with a hand clap. When students clap, they say the word. In this way, the phonemes are brought back together to make a word. For example, *flip* would be modeled *fff-lll-iii-p,* (clap) *flip!*

Zap the Sounds

There are many possibilities for showing phonemic segmentation through physical actions. In Wilson Reading, for example, students tap out sounds using the fingers and thumb. The kindergarten teachers I worked with teach a different action, which they call zapping. After students stretch the word, they zap the sounds. Later, when students are more in tune with paying attention to the sounds of a word, they won't need to stretch. They'll just zap.

To model zapping, first say the word as you make a fist. Next, segment the word into the sounds you hear, pumping your hand and throwing out a finger for each sound you say. For example, the word *it* gets two pumps. The index finger comes out when you say *i*. The middle finger comes out when you say *t*. Finally, draw your fingers back into a fist, blending the sounds together and saying the word.

When giving words, it is important for you to say each word and have your students repeat it before the zapping begins. In this way, you model the correct pronunciation of the word before segmenting the sounds, and your students have the opportunity to repeat that correct pronunciation. After all, a sound-letter speller can't spell an unknown word correctly if it isn't pronounced correctly.

Here is an example of a teaching routine I ran during spelling time. If I used six or seven words, it took about five minutes. My instruction was direct, explicit, and fast paced. The point was to work in lots of practice so the kids could master the technique. Once they had mastered it, they could use it as an independent strategy for spelling and reading unknown monosyllabic words later in the year. In this lesson, we'll pretend the teacher is working with a group of second graders on *r*-controlled syllables.

Teacher: This lesson is about spelling *r*-controlled sounds. What is this lesson about, everyone?

Students: Spelling *r*-controlled sounds!

Teacher: The *ar* sound is spelled *a-r*. How is the *ar* sound spelled, everyone?

Students: *a-r*.

Teacher: The *or* sound is spelled *o-r*. How is the *or* sound spelled, everyone?

Students: *o-r*.

Teacher: Watch me as I zap out the word *stork*. Stork! [Say the word and make a fist.] /s/ /t/ /or/ /k/ [Pump hand, putting out a finger for each phoneme]. Stork! [Pull fingers back into a fist.] Watch: I'll do it one more time. [Repeat the process.]

Teacher: Now I am going to spell each sound with a letter or a group of letters. [Write letters as you say the sounds.] Now I go back and check by reading the word. Stork!

Teacher: Now you try it. Your first word is *card*. Say it.

Students: Card! [They make a fist.]

Teacher: Zap it.

Students: /c/ /ar/ /d/. [They pump their hand and throw out a finger for each sound, ending with index, middle, and ring fingers out. Then they draw their fingers back into a fist and say the word again.] Card!

Teacher: Write it. [Teacher pauses while students write the word.]

Teacher: Check your answer. The word *card* is spelled *c-a-r-d*. Correct your answer if you need to. If your word is correct and you want to put a star next to it, do so. [Students check, correct, and make a star.]

Teacher: Our next word is *born*. [Teacher repeats routine.]

Feel Your Chin Drop

Hearing individual sounds and assigning a letter to each one is not an especially efficient or accurate method for spellers encountering complex multisyllabic words. Just think of trying to segment and spell the word *kindergarten* at the individual sound level, not the syllable level. But by placing their hand under their chin, saying a target word softly and slowly, and counting the number of times their hand moves (which is equivalent to the number of times their chin drops), students can break words into syllables. Then they can stretch or zap the sounds in each syllable to spell the sounds. Still later, they can apply knowledge of patterns and meanings to help them decide how to spell each syllable of an unknown word.

To model the chin drop, place the tips of your fingers, with your palm down, firmly against the edge of your chin. Say the target word slowly but naturally. Start with words that cause a deep drop in your chin, such as *time, phone,* and *slap.* You can also say word parts or "nonsense" words, such as *ipe, oke,* and *ame.*

Tell your students how many times your hand moved and why it moved: every syllable has a vowel, and vowels make our chins move downward when we say them. Sometimes the movement is large, and sometimes it's small. By the way, this is why I greatly prefer the chin drop to the hand clap. Mouths and chins move naturally and unerringly with syllables. Claps do not.

Once you have practiced one-syllable words, move on to two-syllable words. Choose words that produce a definite chin drop: *toenail, highway, snowman,* and so on. Have your students repeat the words with you. Next say three- and four-syllable words: *volcano, condensation.* Finally, mix up the words and, after each pronunciation, ask your students how many syllables they felt. Ask older children or children who are more phonemically advanced to identify the second syllable in a three-syllable word, or the first. All of this draws attention to the sounds in words at the syllable level.

Stretching, zapping, and feeling your chin drop develop phonemic awareness, which is beneficial for students in the early stages of spelling development as well as for those who lag behind in reading, writing, and spelling. Reporting on its meta-analysis of research studies, the National Reading Panel clearly stated that teaching phonemic awareness helps not only preschoolers, kindergartners, and first graders learn to read, but also older readers with reading problems (NICHD 2000).

With short bursts of repeated practice, your students will master the art of stretching, zapping, and chin drops in just a few short weeks. If you regularly review these techniques, it will come as no surprise when later in the year you see students during independent reading or writing time silently mouthing words with their hands under their chins or pumping their fists and throwing out their fingers.

Use a Word You Know: Spell by Analogy

Once students are applying letters and groups of letters to sounds, they are ready to move toward recognizing and applying letter patterns within words. When students are in this developmental stage, they are ready for spelling by analogy.

Put in kid-friendly language, spelling by analogy is using a word you know to spell a word you don't know. Spellers who use this strategy ask questions such as

"Does the word I want to spell sound like a word I already know?" and "Can I use a pattern from a word I know to spell a word I don't know?" If students are asking these questions, they are paying attention to words at the pattern level.

Paying attention to patterns is super-important, because when children pay attention to and remember patterns in words, they can use their acquired knowledge to spell unknown words. For example, a child who has studied and learned *tile* and *mile* can use knowledge of the *ile* pattern to spell the words *file* and *agile*. Likewise, knowledge of the Latin root *ject* can be used to spell the unknown words *project* and *object*. And putting all that knowledge together helps a child spell *projectile*.

On the flip side, readers can use analogy to read unknown words. The word *guile* is decodable if a student is familiar with the *ile* pattern from words such as *tile* and *smile*, and the sound of *gu* in words such as *gun*, *gut*, and *gum*. At a more advanced level, the word *quatrain* is decodable if the reader can see the known word *train* and recall a known word such as *quad* to help decode the *qua* chunk.

Here's the spelling-by-analogy strategy, step-by-step. Teach it, and writers will have a plan for spelling unknown words:

1. Say the word you want to spell out loud. If it is a lengthy word, put your hand under your chin and say the word. Feel your chin move for each syllable.

2. Ask yourself, *Do I know of another word or another syllable that sounds like this word or syllable? Do I hear any word patterns or families I know?*

3. Write down the letter patterns that correspond with what you are hearing.

4. Check the word after you spell it: Do the patterns you see match what you hear? Can you use rhyming words or syllables you know to check this word? Does your word *look* like it's spelled correctly?

Spelling by analogy—using patterns in known words to spell unknown words—is taught and developed when you model the strategy during instruction, and through activities such as Look Touch Say, word sorts, and word dictation. When modeling how to spell by analogy, use a think-aloud to bring your inner thinking to light. You might say something like this to your class of first or second graders:

"I want to write the sentence *I like to visit my friends in Pittsburgh.* First I write *I like to.* I know how to spell all of these words. Next comes the word *visit. I like to visit.* If I put my fingers under my chin, I feel two syllables when I say *visit.*

The first syllable I hear and feel is *vis*. *Vis* sounds like a word I know—*his*. *His* is spelled *h-i-s*. So I'm going to spell *vis v-i-s*. I'm using a word I know to spell a syllable I don't know.

"I'm going to say *visit* again. *Vis-it*. The second syllable is *it*. That one is easy—*i-t*. Now I'm going to read the whole word and see if the letters match the sounds: *visit*.

"The next part of my sentence is *my friends. I like to visit my friends.* I know how to spell *my* and I know how to spell *friend* because of the saying 'a friend to the end.'

"The last part of my sentence is *in Pittsburgh*. Spelling *in* is easy for me. What about *Pittsburgh*? When I put my fingers under my chin, I feel two syllables. *Pitts, burgh. Pitts* sounds like *hits, h-i-t-s,* and *sits, s-i-t-s,* so I am going to spell this syllable *P-i-t-s*. The *P* is uppercase because Pittsburgh is a special place. Next is *burgh*. That sounds like *bird*, which is spelled *b-i-r-d*. So I'll spell *burgh b-i-r-g*. Now I go back and read the word. *Pitsbirg*. Hmm . . . That doesn't look right to me. In fact, it looks funny! When I close my eyes, I see a *u* in the last syllable, not an *i*. So I'm going to change it to *Pitsburg*. That looks a lot better to me. Now I am probably close. But I might not be 100 percent correct. So I am going to circle this word and look it up or ask for help later."

In a one-syllable word, the spelling pattern that consists of the vowel and all the letters that follow it is known by any number of names, including chunk, family, and, if you're a linguist, rime. Regardless of what it is called—chunk, family, rime—a spelling pattern such as *ack* or *ile* helps students understand how words work and how patterns can be used to create words. In Chapter 4 we saw the thirty-seven high-frequency phonograms that many teachers present to young children. These patterns can be used to create hundreds of words. An even more powerful organizational scheme for spelling patterns is the seven syllable types, which we'll discuss at length toward the end of the chapter.

One last thing about teaching students to spell by analogy: it makes sense to fold in instruction on spelling principles. In Chapter 3 we discussed how some traditional spelling principles, such as "certain vowel team patterns are almost always pronounced the same way" and "the position of a sound often determines its spelling," are broadly applicable. For example, many sound spellings are position dependent, including *oi* (*toil* and *toy*), *ou* (*out* and *how*), and *s* (*sad* and *mess*). The *k* sound is another example. Although sometimes spelled with a *k* at the beginning of a word (for example, *kite, kale, kitten*), a beginning *k* sound is more likely to be spelled with a *c* (*cat, crazy, cantaloupe*), and it is almost always spelled with a *ck* at the end of a short-vowel, one-syllable word (for example, *tick, black, snuck, crock, backpack*).

The point about principles is that like the patterns themselves, spelling principles are specific, stable, and predictable over large numbers of words. If you repeatedly present them and model their use, your students will begin to see how the majority of word spellings are both knowable and unsurprising. As Louisa Moats says, "These principles provide a framework for understanding those seemingly endless lists of rules that have given English spelling its bad reputation" (2005/2006, 5).

Think About the Meaning of the Word or Word Part

Just as words have sound parts (phonemes) and letter parts (graphemes), they also have meaning parts (morphemes). Teach morphemes to students, and they can use them to spell unknown words based on meaning.

One-syllable words are often morphemes unto themselves. Think of words that rhyme or sound similar, words such as *two* and *too* and *our* and *hour*. Even at a young age, students can be taught to pay attention to the meaning of these words. But the initial teaching must be direct and explicit, and some children need several opportunities for practice. In Figure 5.3 we see a third grader who is confused about the usage of the word *are*. I know that the third-grade teacher, who happens to be me, didn't give enough opportunities to practice the use of both *are* and *our*. So I'm not surprised that this third-grade writer didn't use the word correctly in her independently written piece. As an instructional guru once said, "If they didn't learn it, you didn't teach it!"

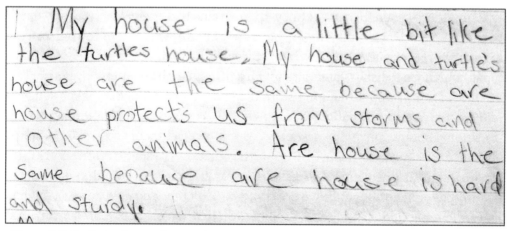

Figure 5.3 Confusing the words *are* and *our*

In the fourth, fifth, and sixth grades, affixes and Latin roots take center stage in spelling, and it's at this time that teaching children to pay attention to meaning really begins to pay off. Most upper-grade elementary school teachers I know spend a good deal of time teaching students prefix and suffix meanings, such as *un* (not), *uni* (one), *less* (without), and so on.

Exploring Latin and Greek base words and root words helps students understand that word spellings hold word meanings. In the upper grades, spelling instruction shares a lot with vocabulary instruction because so much of it is meaning based. By examining the spellings of seemingly unrelated words, children can begin to see how and why words are actually related to one another. For example, *astro* and *aster* have their roots in *astron*, the Greek word for "star." Knowing the morpheme *aster* helps readers understand the meaning of *aster* (the flower) and *asterisk*. But what about *disaster*? *Disaster*, a word that literally means "bad star," is rooted in the ancient belief that comets (once thought to be stars) were harbingers of bad news. When a comet appeared, war, pestilence, or some other calamity was sure to follow.

Here's another interesting connection between common words with the root *quar*. We all know a *quart* is a fourth of a gallon, a *quarter* is a fourth of a dollar, and a *quartet* has four members. But what's *quarantine's* connection to four? Turns out, *quarantine* comes from *quarante* or *quarania*, the French and Italian words for forty. In the days of sailing ships, if a vessel arriving in port was suspected of harboring an infectious disease, the ship and its sailors had to avoid contact with others by staying moored offshore for forty days.

Paying attention to meaning can be especially helpful to spellers because the sound (but not the spelling) of a morpheme can change between words. If students understand that *know* is spelled *k-n-o-w*, and realize that the meaning of the word *knowledge* is related to *know*, they can use that information to correctly spell the word *knowledge*, even though the word's initial vowel sound is different from the vowel sound in *know*. The same holds true for word derivations such as *pray* and *prayer*, *define* and *definite*, *wild* and *wilderness*, and *relate* and *relative*. I use the "think about meaning" strategy fairly frequently. For example, because I have a hard time seeing the word *competition* in my mind, sometimes I'll spell it *compitition*. But as soon as I write it, I can see that it doesn't look right. But if I remember to start my spelling process by thinking of the word *compete*, which is easy for me to see and spell, then I spell *competition* correctly right from the start.

Using meaning to spell a word is like one of those principles mentioned earlier. Spellings of roots and base words often remain stable across word derivations, even as the sounds of the roots and base words change. Using meaning to spell is also like spelling by analogy. In effect, students can use a word they know to help them spell a word they don't know. This works in reading, too, for recognizing and knowing the meaning of a root or base enables readers to decode and understand other words that incorporate the word part. Thus, decoding and meaning can be achieved through analogy, just as in spelling.

As before, teach your students a little routine for spelling an unknown word by analogy:

5. Say the long word you want to spell out loud. Think about what it means.

6. Ask yourself, *Is there a shorter word that is related to the meaning of this word? Do I know of a short word that would help me spell this longer word?*

7. Write down the short word you know. Use it to spell the longer word.

8. Check the word after you spell it: Is most or all of the spelling of the short word contained in the longer word? Does your longer word *look* like it's spelled correctly?

Use a Mnemonic

If you need a mnemonic to remember how to spell *mnemonic*, then just like me, you are not the world's best speller. I have an especially hard time committing words to my brain dictionary if they originate in a language such as French, whose phoneme-grapheme relationships are confusing to me. For words I can't see in my mind or break down into common sound-spelling patterns—words such as *camouflage, ricocheted,* and *silhouette*—I use a mnemonic.

A mnemonic device is a pattern of letters, an idea, or an association that aids memory and recall. You can encourage children to generate mnemonics for words they commonly misspell. The first step is to help them be metacognitive. Students must be aware that some words are difficult for them. Therefore, they must pay attention to what those words are. The second step is to encourage them to have a few spelling and memory tricks up their sleeves.

Although you can teach one mnemonic to your entire class, it's better to let students come up with their own way of remembering a word. Individualized mnemonics work best because what makes sense to one student won't make sense to another. A mnemonic can take any shape or form, as long as its usage results in a correctly spelled word.

One trick is to say the word "in a silly way." By *silly* I mean pronounce silent letters, unaccented syllables, and non-English pronunciations as if they follow typical, common English pronunciations. Before the word *camouflage* became part of my brain dictionary (through repeated practice spelling it), I had to use a mnemonic to spell it correctly. I would say, "cam-ou-flage," with the *ou* pronounced as in *you* and the *flage* pronounced as if it rhymed with *rage*. To spell *ricocheted*, I have to say, "ric-o-chet-ed," and I visualize the patterns *ric, o, chet,* and *ed* in my mind as I say them.

In the past, some of my fifth graders used silly pronunciations to help them remember how to spell difficult words. To help them spell *conscience,* some pronounced it *con-science.* Together we pronounced *environment* as if my friend Ron were stuck in the middle—*en-vi-Ron-ment.* I remember that one of the better words, at least for fifth graders, was *pee-neumonia,* which, of course, is *pneumonia.* Kids can also string words into a sentence, which makes the pronunciation more ridiculous. "While walking in the en-vi-Ron-ment, I caught pee-neumonia!"

It's important that students follow their funny pronunciation with the actual pronunciation. You want to make sure they are learning the mnemonic, not the wrong way of pronouncing the word. To help themselves spell the words *calendar* and *Wednesday,* students might say, "I looked at the cal-en-darr and saw it was Wed-ness-day." But when they read it back to themselves, they should read, "I looked at the calendar and saw it was Wednesday."

Creating visuals that match a word's syllables is another mnemonic device kids can use. Adults can employ them, too. To spell *silhouette,* I think of "the outline of a girl who lives in a silly house." *Silly* helps me remember *sil, house* triggers *hou,* and *girl* helps me remember the diminutive/feminine ending *ette,* as in *majorette* and *brunette.* Fourth or fifth graders might remember *raspberry* as "a raspy berry" or *attendance* by saying, "*At ten,* I can *dance.*" I still remember a few from my elementary school days: "A *friend* to the *end*" and "The *principal* is your *pal.*" Each helped me spell a word that was difficult to remember.

See the Word Inside Your Head

Seeing the word inside your head is the strategy accomplished spellers use most often. Some children develop this skill naturally. Others do not. To encourage students to build and use the dictionaries in their brains, teach them to study their words using the strategy given below. Then, when it comes time to spell words independently during writing (or on a test), remind kids to use this part of the strategy: see the word in your mind, write the word, and check the word. As teachers, we hope that "see-write-check" generalizes into the automatic ability to visualize a word, write it down, and then check it against the word stored in the brain dictionary.

I have seen variations of the "see the word" strategy for a couple of decades now. My most recent encounter was while reading through the *Spelling Connections Teacher Manual* (Gentry 2016a), which presents a three-step strategy for studying spelling words. I offer this two-step variation instead:

1. Say-See, Hide-See

   a. When studying your word, first say the word. Then say the letters in the word. As you say the letters, group the letters into patterns that you know.

   b. Put the word into your brain. Use the smartphone in your mind and snap a picture. Post the picture! Can you see it?

   c. Hide the word you are studying. This means cover it with your hand, close your book, close your eyes, or turn your paper over.

   d. See the word in your head (look at the picture you posted). See the letters and patterns that make up the word.

2. Write, Check (and Correct)

   a. Write the word. As you write, think of the letters and patterns that make up the word.

   b. Check your spelling against the spelling in the book or on your paper. If you made a mistake, correct it.

   c. Then look at the correct spelling and say the correct spelling, chunking it into groups and patterns like you did before.

What follows is an example of how I might model my use of this strategy and use a think-aloud to explain its workings:

MW: This week's lesson is about words with the *e-r* ending. What is this week's lesson about, everyone?

Students: Words with the *e-r* ending.

MW: I am going to model how I use our spelling study strategy to study some of the words you might have on your list. So listen as I think out loud. [Pointing to the word *speaker* on the whiteboard]. My first word to study is *speaker*. Our strategy says, "Say, See." I look at the word and say it. Then

I see letters in the word and chunk them into patterns I know: *sp-eak-er*. *Speaker*. I see those chunks in my mind. [Covering the word with sheet of paper.] Next, our strategy says, "Hide and See." I've hidden the word and I'm closing my eyes. I'm seeing the word spelled out in chunks in my mind. [Closes eyes and silently mouths, *sp-eak-er, speaker*.] Next, I write the word. [Writes the word on the board.] Finally, I check the word. [Uncovers the original word.] Let's see: *sp-eak-er, speaker*. Perfect! I have nothing to correct. Another way to remember a word is to break it into meaning parts. Here's a new word: *dreamer*. What's the word, everyone?

Students: *Dreamer*!

MW: I see it is made up of the base word *dream*, plus the *er* ending, which means "one who dreams." What does *dreamer* mean, everyone?

Students: "One who dreams."

MW: By the way, what does *speaker* mean?

[Some students raise their hands. Two blurt out, "'One who speaks'!"]

MW: Put your hands down and think for five seconds. What does *speaker* mean? [Waits three seconds.] Tell someone at your elbow.

Students: [They turn and talk to a peer sitting next to an elbow.]

MW: If you said, "one who speaks," then you are correct. The first step of my spelling study strategy is to Say-See, Hide-See. I say the word and see the chunks. I can see this word as *dream*, which is the base word, and *er*, which is the ending. *Dream-er, dreamer*. [Covering the word with sheet of paper.] Now I Hide and See. I close my eyes and see the two chunks of meaning in my mind. [Closes eyes and silently mouths *dream-er, dreamer*.] Next, I write the word. [Writes the word on the board.] Finally, I check it. [Uncovers the original word.] Let's see: *dream-er, dreamer*. Yep, that's it.

The more students read, read, read and write, write, write, the more words they regularly encounter and the better their chances of moving words into their brain dictionaries. Therefore, I encourage you to make and keep space for students to engage in extended bouts of reading and writing. And here's something else to consider: although one child may easily store a word in his or her brain and then visualize it, another may not, even when repeatedly exposed to the word. If you have students who cannot easily store and see a word inside their heads, then encourage them to use other strategies, ones that play to their strengths, such as spelling by analogy, thinking about word meaning, and even circling the word and using a spell checker to correct it.

Get Close, Circle, Correct

When it comes to spelling words while writing, students need to hear that "all writers make mistakes" and "writers work to fix their mistakes." Writers, both children and adults, can use their metacognitive ability to know their spelling strengths and weaknesses, know when they don't know how to spell a word, and purposefully use a strategy to ensure that a word is spelled correctly.

The first thing we can teach student writers is that they should be aware that when they write, some of their words will probably be misspelled. But awareness is only the first step. Spellers need to take action to navigate past their spelling bumps and fill their spelling potholes.

One of my favorite "take action" strategies is "circle the word." If you teach this, you'll really put spelling responsibility on your students. The strategy has three parts:

1. Spell the word as best you can

2. circle the word if you're still uncertain and

3. go back and correct your circled words (or verify that they are spelled correctly).

To teach this strategy, model writing in front of your class, and engage in a think-aloud that explains how you think about spelling as you write. The following language might help you teach this strategy. Say some version of it during your instruction:

- "Writers sometimes don't know how to spell words they want to write. If you struggle to spell words as you write, don't worry. And don't spend too much time trying to figure out the spelling. Spell the word as best you can and then circle it. Then keep writing. At first it's important to focus more on writing and less on spelling, because writers work to get their thoughts down while the thoughts are still fresh in their minds."

- "When you are finished writing, go back and reread for spelling. Circle any word that doesn't 'look right' to you, or any word that you think might be spelled incorrectly."

- "Correct the spelling of a circled word or verify that it is spelled correctly. This is what that means:

- "Cross-check the sounds you hear in the word against the letters and patterns you have written. Stretch your syllables so that you hear all the sounds. Check your word: are you spelling all of the sounds?

- "When you think you are close to the correct spelling of a word, type your word into a spell checker. If the spell checker gives you back a word that you *know* is not the word you want, try spelling your original word a different way. Think about your patterns and about spelling by analogy. Finally, ask a friend or a teacher to confirm that your spelling is the correct spelling.

- When you think you are close to the correct spelling of a word, see if you can find the word in your writing dictionary. If this is too difficult, ask a friend or a teacher to help you. Once you have the word, cross-check your spelling with the dictionary spelling. If the words are spelled the same, give yourself a pat on the back. If your word is different from the dictionary word, correct your word to match the dictionary word."

If you teach kindergarten or first grade, simply provide the correct spelling of the word for your students instead of having children circle words and then look them up in a dictionary. You can provide the correct spelling with underwriting (writing under the child's word), as shown in Figure 5.4. For older students, such as students in second through fifth grade, try writing words in a writer's dictionary or the spelling section of a writing journal (see Figure 5.5). If a student is working hard to get close to a correct spelling, but the spelling is still too far off to be easily found in a writing dictionary or corrected by

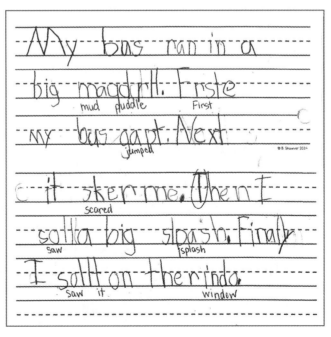

Figure 5.4 Teacher underwriting

Figure 5.5 Teacher-supplied words in writing dictionary

a spell checker, then simply provide the correct spelling. The goal is to have a "not too loose, not too tight" philosophy. You want your students to take responsibility for using strategies and trying to correct their misspellings, but you don't want to frustrate struggling readers by having them plow through a dictionary of words they can't read to find a word they don't know how to spell.

At first, your students may fail to use the "circle the word and correct it" strategy, especially if you have been spelling unknown words for them. But don't lose heart. Keep modeling the strategy, keep your expectations high, and don't give in to automatically spelling words for them when they ask, "How do you spell ____?" Expect students to regularly circle words (Figure 5.6) and then use a strategy or two to try to correct them. If you have children who regularly spell 99 or 100 percent of their written words correctly, then ask them to circle at least two words just to practice the strategy, and challenge them to use more advanced, interesting, and difficult-to-spell words in their writing. Finally, you may have to set a minimum or a ceiling on the number of words circled. For students who misspell several words but never circle any, provide a minimum number of words to aim for, saying something such as, "I expect to see four words circled in every piece of writing." And for students who circle ten or fifteen words, set an upper limit so they're not focusing exclusively on this strategy. Perhaps you could say, "You are working very hard to practice our strategy. Thank you for your effort. But I want you to practice using only five words. If you circle and correct five words, I know you are really trying."

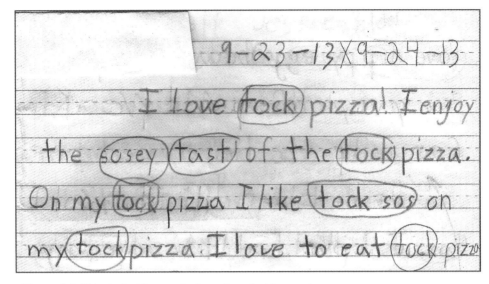

Figure 5.6 This student knows she has misspelled *taco* and *sauce*.

Teaching Seven Syllable Types

The scope and sequence of a spelling program is typically organized loosely around the developmental stages of spelling and the word features associated with each stage. For example, most scope and sequences for first-grade children, who are developing the ability to match letters to the sounds they hear, concentrate on teaching CVC patterns, consonant blends, digraphs, and CV*e* patterns. In contrast, a scope and sequence for third graders, who are developing the ability to notice and use patterns in words, typically contains lessons on frequent and infrequent vowel sounds and spellings, inflectional endings (where plurals and tenses are formed), and special consonant spellings such as *soft c* and *soft g*, as well as suffixes, prefixes, and homophones. As the stages of spelling development progress, more and more spelling features are added. Take a minute to look over the scope and sequence of any spelling program for grades one to five, and you will see dozens of spelling features listed.

Because these many features are not strongly organized into a few broad categories that are easy to understand and teach, they can present real difficulties for both teachers and students. First, a weakly organized scope makes it harder for teachers to answer these questions: "which features have my students mastered, which features need to be retaught, which features do my students have control of when they write, and which features are my students seeing and controlling when they decode as they read?"

Second, when teachers have an overwhelming number of spelling features to think about, they may lose sight of these big-picture reasons for teaching spelling: spelling is for building the brain dictionary, spelling is to enable fluent writing, spelling is for strengthening decoding, and so on. Also, a focus on the minute details (dozens of features) gives teachers and students the false notion that English spellings are unruly, nonsensical, and impossible to predict. Finally, teaching spelling as a weekly stream of loosely categorized features makes it harder for children to learn and remember, and harder for teachers to teach efficiently and effectively. For example, if you were asked to teach third graders to recall, in any order, the numbers and letters of these two sets—*2, 7, 3, 5, 1, 6, 8, 4* and *b, e, h, t, e, h, c, n, g, e, a*—how would you choose to teach them? Would you teach them as unorganized strings of numbers and letters—*2, 7, 3, 5, 1, 6, 8, 4* and *b, e, h, t, e, h, c, n, g, e, a*—or would you teach them as organized groups: *2468-1357* and *Be the change*? Obviously, the latter.

It pays to organize, through categorization, large sets of information into smaller subsets. Fortunately for us, a handy categorization method exists. It's called syllable types. Syllable types provide an overarching instructional strategy by categorizing all syllables into seven categories, thus reining in the number of spelling features and the breadth of a typical spelling scope and sequence. With only seven types of patterns to teach, your spelling instruction can be more focused and powerful. And when children master the knowledge and use of the syllable types, they have a master plan (a strategy) for decoding during reading and encoding during spelling.

In my second or third year of teaching, when I first learned that there was a way to simplify my basal program's complex spelling scope and sequence, that I could organize all the parts of my spelling instruction into seven easy-to-understand categories, and that I could save time even as I engaged in more powerful teaching, it was like a giant 400-watt light bulb had suddenly been turned on over my head. I was thrilled. That bulb is still burning, and it's burning over the heads of others, too. I regularly talk with teachers who gush about using syllable types to teach phonics and spelling in their classrooms. I think we all get so excited about them because syllable types draw attention to all that lies at the heart of spelling: sounds, patterns, and meaning. And when students' attention is drawn to the heart of the matter, they are in a much better position to use the strategies we discussed earlier, to build a dictionary in their brains, and to become more fluent readers and writers.

The seven categories of syllable types can be taught by teachers and used by students between and across grade levels. It seems to me that any strategy, routine, or method of organization that crosses classrooms and grade levels holds the possibility of greater and longer-lasting student learning. Simply put, when students experience and use a strategy, routine, or method year after year from a multitude of teachers, they are much more likely to master that strategy, routine, or method and consistently apply it in a variety of settings.

Finally, teaching spelling via syllable types drives home the encoding-decoding, spelling-reading connection. It allows you to completely align your phonics scope and sequence with your spelling scope and sequence. Equally important, it improves a struggling student's ability to read and spell multisyllabic words because it is one tool (breaking words into syllables) that provides repeated practice in two areas: spelling (encoding) and reading (decoding).

One thing before we move on: Researchers and writers present differing views on spelling nomenclature. For example, some folks call *ar, ir,* and *or* patterns vowel-*r* syllables, and others call them *r*-controlled syllables. Likewise, there are differences in opinion about how to classify patterns such as *ore* (*store*) and *air* (*stair*). Are they *r*-controlled? Or is one a vowel-consonant-*e* syllable and the other a vowel-team syllable? I mention differences of opinion because I present syllable types as seven in number, whereas spelling experts such as Louisa Moats and Barbara Wilson present them as six. But in the grand scheme of spelling and reading, these differences are minor. The important point is to organize spelling features into categories of syllable types and then teach them well, over time, in spelling, reading, and writing.

Teach What a Syllable Is

If you are going to organize your spelling around syllable types, I suggest you first teach what a syllable is. Begin with the idea that a syllable is a word or a part of a word that has at least one vowel in it. The vowel in every syllable causes your chin to drop when you say the vowel sound. Demonstrate and practice this by using all that we talked about in the chin-drop strategy section.

Introduce the Seven Syllable Types

Once your students have a basic understanding of what a syllable is (a word or a word part that causes their chin to drop because it has at least one vowel in it), introduce the syllable types. Figure 5.7 shows each syllable type, along with an explanation, examples, and, if applicable, exceptions.

Syllable Type	Explanation	Examples	Exceptions
Closed	The vowel sound is typically a pure short sound or a nasalized short sound. The syllable has a single vowel followed by one or more consonants.	cat, best, strap, moss ham, thanking robin, puppet fantastic, athletic	*ild* as in *wild* *ind* as in *find* *ost* as in *most*
Open	The vowel sound is typically long. The syllable ends with a single vowel that is not closed in by a consonant.	go, no, he, she, flu, shy lady, baby, ruby hero, zero potato	Schwa sounds: *a* as in *Alaska* *e* as in *the* *i* as in *president*
Vowel-Consonant-*e*	The vowel sound is typically long. The syllable ends with a vowel, consonant, and silent *e*.	plate, hike, Rome, tube lifetime, grapevine	give, live, love, motive notice, novice garbage, baggage
Vowel Team	The syllable contains two adjacent vowels, or the syllable contains a vowel-consonant combination (*igh, ew, ow*).	green, throat, plain cloud, moon, toy chew, high, flow rainbow, headway	
***R*-controlled**	The syllable contains a vowel plus an *r*. The vowel sound is not long, short, or a variant. The syllable is not VCe, such as *stare*, *hire*, or *store*. The syllable is not a vowel team plus an *r*, such as *fear*, *deer*, or *pair*.	horn, sort star, barn, card germ, fern, jerk third, shirt, dirt hurt, burn, murder corner, farmer barnyard surgery	
Consonant-*le*	The syllable contains a consonant plus the letters *l* and *e*. The syllable is final, occurring only at the end of a multisyllabic word.	table, rifle, bugle puzzle, ripple people	
Stable Final (leftovers)	Found in multisyllabic words, this syllable type consists of a number of different ending sets: *al, el* *sion, tion* *ture, sure*	regal, annual duffel, angel fusion, explosion nation, education nature, future pleasure, composure	

Figure 5.7 Seven syllable types

Now you may be thinking, *You said there were seven syllable types. But there are exceptions in each category. Spelling is so confusing!* Although I can't deny that exceptions add complexity to the simplicity of just seven syllable types, I maintain that when you tell students, "We are going to group all of our spelling patterns into seven basic types," you have focused a sprawling topic, making it much easier to understand and easier for children to notice commonalities and differences among its many parts.

To further illustrate this point, Figure 5.8 shows the thirty-seven high-frequency phonograms (discussed in Chapter 4, Figure 4.1) grouped by syllable type. You can see how each falls into one of three syllable types: closed, VC*e*, and vowel team.

Syllable Type	Phonogram					
Closed	ack	an	ank	ap	ash	at
	ell	est	ick	ill	in	ing
	ink	ip	it	ock	op	ot
	uck	ug	ump	unk		
VCe	ake	ale	ame	ate	ice	ide
	ine	oke	ore			
Vowel Team	ail	ain	aw	ay	eat	ight

Figure 5.8 The thirty-seven high-frequency phonograms categorized by syllable type

By the way, this sequence of syllable type—closed, VC*e*, and vowel team—is an appropriate sequence of instruction for students in first grade, keeping in mind that those who do not master the closed-syllable type will need to be instructed until they do. Open syllables and *r*-controlled syllables can be added in the second-grade sequence. By the end of third grade, students will be ready to begin organizing spelling words around all seven types.

Use Syllable Types Across Space and Time

The seven syllable types give schools an organizing principle that crosses grade levels, providing a common language for all teachers of reading, writing, and spelling. At the same time, seven syllable types provide an organizing framework that all students can use to better understand the workings of spelling features in every spelling stage, from consonants, digraphs, and short vowels in the early-alphabetic stage to long vowel teams and variant vowel teams in the patterns-within-words stage, to roots, affixes, and inflected endings in the meaning stage.

If a school were to embrace the teaching of syllable types, students would have three years of exposure to this organizing principle by the time they got to fourth grade, surely a strong foundation. And even in the final stage of spelling development, where the focus is meaning rather than pattern, syllable patterns can be referenced and explored. For example, Figure 5.9 shows how multisyllabic words are made up of combinations of syllable types, and Figure 5.10 shows how words presented in the fourth-grade long *u* master list (from Figure 4.4) can also be presented and understood as a string of connected syllable types.

Combine Syllable Types to Spell and Read Hundreds of Words!

Syllable Type	Two-Syllable Words	Three-Syllable Words	Four-Syllable Words
Open and **Closed**	react, frozen, pretend, topaz, pilot	microchip, coconut, develop	microcosmic, hemoglobin
Closed and **Open**	bingo, tango, candy	volcano, tuxedo, alfresco, Han Solo*	economy, humility
Open and **VCe**	define, rotate, skyline, biplane	microwave, patronize	locomotive
Closed and **VCe**	endgame, textile, explode, cellphone	compensate, valentine, tranquilize	administrate, disenfranchise
Closed, **Open**, and **VCe**		advocate, obsolete, gramophone, educate	congratulate, monopolize
***R*-controlled** and **Closed**	farming, cornhusk, firmest, burlap	government, tarnishing	caterpillar

*Two words, three syllables, and high interest!

Figure 5.9 Multisyllabic words are made of syllable types.

Long *u* Spelled *ew*, *ui*

Word	Syllables	Syllable Types
chew	chew	vowel team
fruit	fruit	vowel team
dewdrop	dew-drop	vowel team–closed
suitcase	suit-case	vowel team–VCe
fruitcake	fruit-cake	vowel team–VCe
renewing	re-new-ing	open–vowel team–closed
confusing	con-fu-sing	closed–open–closed

Figure 5.10 Spelling list organized by syllable types

As syllable types are introduced over time—in each teacher's classroom during a school year and in each grade level, year after school year—students can explore longer and longer words made from a mixture of short syllable types. This exploration of and exposure to multisyllabic words increases their ability to successfully read and write hundreds if not thousands, of words.

Teacher Comments for Students' Spelling Questions

For me, teaching can be an exercise in keeping my wits about me. On my brain-is-fuzzy bad days, I'm a step behind the students and lacking in quick and easy solutions to their reading or writing difficulties. But on my good days, my responses are right at the tip of my tongue. If you are having a brain-is-fuzzy bad day, use the language in Figure 5.11 to reinforce the spelling strategies you've taught when students pepper you with questions and complaints.

When a Student Says . . .	You Say . . .
How do you spell ___?	What strategy or strategies did you use to try to spell it? Did you use your sounds and letters? Did you apply a pattern that matches the sounds? Can you use a word you know to help you spell your word? Find the syllables in this word, think about the syllable types we have learned, and then try to spell the syllables using your knowledge of syllable types. I'd like you to try to spell it yourself. Use a strategy to get close to the right spelling. Then circle the word and correct it when you are finished writing.
Is this word spelled correctly?	What do you think? Does it look right to you? No, it isn't spelled correctly, but you have some of its sounds and patterns spelled correctly. Some of your syllables are spelled correctly, but some are not. Here are the syllables that are correct. Think about how to correct the other syllables. It's close to correct. Did you check your spelling with the dictionary or a spell-checker? Did you ask a friend? Wow, that word *is* spelled correctly! How did you figure out how to spell it?
I don't have any misspelled words in my sentences!	Even the best writers make spelling mistakes. Pick two words that are complex, and check them to make sure they are correct. It's best to double-check your most difficult words with a dictionary or spell-checker just to make sure. Which words *may* not be correct? I want you to find three words that may not be correct and check them with a dictionary or spell-checker. You said the same thing before, but when I checked your writing, I found four misspelled words. I want you to find four words in your writing that are more difficult to spell, circle them, and then check them with a dictionary.
My word isn't in the dictionary. My spell-checker is giving me the wrong word. Is this word on my spell-checker the word I want?	Your spelling is close but not close enough. Your word is spelled with ___. Look for this ___ word part in the dictionary. Put this spelling into your spell-checker. You're right, it isn't in the dictionary! Your word is spelled ___. Write this spelling down in your writer's dictionary and use it the next time you want to write this word.

Figure 5.11 Teacher responses to student questions and comments

What's Next?

It's time to connect the strategies that students use to spell with the words they will spell. We'll connect word lists and spelling strategies through activities that explicitly and directly teach children about sound, pattern, and meaning, as well as activities that allow kids to explore how sound, pattern, and meaning are manifested within words. Once you add teaching activities to your spelling strategies, focused and lengthy master lists, focused scope and sequence, and assessment options, your spelling instruction will be truly transformed.

IF YOU HAVE ONLY TEN MINUTES

You can begin to take action on spelling strategies even if you have only ten minutes.

- Pick a word you often use in writing. Scan through the list of strategies in Figure 5.1. Practice employing each of the strategies to spell that word.

- Identify the spelling development level the majority of your students are on. Then read through the list of spelling strategies in Figure 5.1. Pick the strategy most appropriate for the majority of your students to use. Spend a few minutes thinking about how you might teach this strategy over time, in a number of different lessons.

- Take what you know from the previous paragraph and apply it to a couple of lessons. That is, take ten minutes twice a week for a few weeks and teach your students what the strategy is and how to use it. Employ modeling and a think-aloud in your lesson. Notice when your students use the strategy while spelling and writing.

EXPLORE CONNECTIONS

1. Which strategy would be best suited for making connections to your phonics program? If you teach in an upper grade that doesn't spend a lot of time on phonics, which strategy would be best suited for making connections to vocabulary or comprehension instruction?

2. What is the role of metacognition in reading and spelling? What is the role of metacognition in writing and spelling?

3. Which spelling strategy do you most often use when spelling a word that doesn't come to you automatically? Can you use your knowledge of your personal spelling strategy to inform your instruction? Do you see students in your classroom who don't use the strategy that you most often use?

CHAPTER 6

Teach Activities

IN THIS CHAPTER

- We learn research-based spelling activities that align with the spelling strategies discussed in the previous chapter.

- We see how differentiating activities throughout the year gives students opportunities to practice what is most important in spelling: hearing and spelling sounds, noticing and using patterns, applying meaning, and building a mental repository of words that can be used for reading and writing.

Activities That Reinforce Spelling Strategies

Teaching—what a difficult thing to do! As teachers we must communicate ideas, foster curiosity, engage the disinterested, manage large groups, differentiate for individuals, redirect behaviors, plan lessons, conduct assessments, modify instruction . . . should I go on? The list certainly does, as do the hours and days in which each of these acts must be done competently, professionally, and with a caring heart.

Because the demands of teaching are intense, it's a good idea to use instructional activities that create synergy with the learning strategies we teach and the content we cover. The spelling activities presented in this chapter can help create this synergy. Each provides students with opportunities to practice one or more of the strategies discussed in Chapter 5, such as hearing and spelling sounds, thinking about word meaning, and using a known word to spell an unknown word.

Figure 6.1 displays the activities presented in the chapter. As you read, you'll notice some are direct and explicit. Others are more exploratory and constructivist in nature. Each can be done with a whole group or in small groups, and once the activities are learned, your students can do many of them during independent work time or in centers. Finally, and most importantly, every activity helps students build the skills they need to be capable spellers, writers, and readers.

Activity	Description	Configuration	Materials	Grade
Segment to Spell	Words are spelled using a spelling grid. Each box in the grid stands for a sound. One grapheme (letter or letter combination) goes in each box.	Large group Small group Independent Buddy	Paper, pencil, whiteboards, markers, letter tiles, pattern tiles	late K–2 older struggling students
Word Ladders	Two target words are given on either end of a ladder. Teacher asks students to change one letter in the first word to create a new word. Letters and words keep changing until the last target word is spelled.	Large group Small group Independent with written clues	Paper, pencil, whiteboard, markers, magnetic journal, worksheet	1-3 4-6
Look Touch Say	In this teacher-directed activity, students look for a target word, touch it with a finger, and then say it.	Large group Small group	Word list or word cards	1-6
Word Sorts	Students sort word cards according to teacher directions. Sorts can be open, closed, or a bit of both. This activity is constructive and exploratory in nature.	Large group Small group Independent and Buddy with written directions	Word cards	1-6
Six-Word Storytelling	Students explore the arrangement of six word cards to create a story that uses word meaning appropriately.	Large group Small group	Word cards	1-6
Word Dictation	Teacher dictates a word and students spell it.	Large group Small group Buddy	Paper, pencil, whiteboard, markers, iPad	1-6
Sentence Dictation	Teacher dictates a sentence and students spell it.	Large group Small group	Paper, pencil, whiteboard, markers, iPad	1-6
Flip Folder	Students practice spelling words using the "see the word in your head" strategy.	Buddy Independent	Word cards, slips of paper, manila flip folder	1-6
Practice Test with Instant Error Correction	Teacher gives a short spelling test (five–eight words). After each word, teacher stops and gives correct spelling. Students check and correct using Dot and Circle method. Instruction here is direct and explicit.	Large group Small group Buddy	Paper, pencil, whiteboard, marker	1-6

Figure 6.1 Activities for spelling instruction

Segment to Spell: Using Spelling Grids

Segment to Spell helps children focus on the sounds of words and then spell those sounds by assigning appropriate letters and groups of letters. It also helps children notice and remember patterns. This activity is typically used with the youngest readers and writers, but it is also appropriate for older students who have not yet mastered the alphabetic principle, especially regarding vowel sounds and spellings.

To support spellers in the sound-letter matching process, provide them with spelling grids, often called Elkonin boxes. Each box in a spelling grid represents one phoneme. Students listen to a word, segment the word into individual phonemes, and then fill in the boxes of the grid one sound at a time.

Typically, spelling grids can be purchased as whiteboards (for writing on with erasable markers or for organizing letter tiles) or magnetic boards (for magnetic letter tiles). You can also make your own write-and-erase boxes by printing grids on card stock and laminating them. If you have magnetic letter tiles, you can use steel cookie sheets. Draw your grids with a permanent marker. For young children, use grids with a varying number of boxes. For older children, you can use one grid with five or six boxes. (See Figure 6.2.)

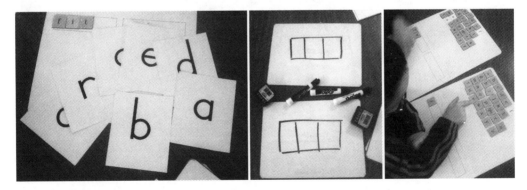

Figure 6.2 Materials for spelling grids

When introducing Segment to Spell, tell your students how many boxes will be filled in. Then follow this routine:

- Say the target word. Have the students repeat the word;
- With the students, stretch the word, zap the word, or do both (as discussed in Chapter 5);

- Have the students fill each box of the grid with the appropriate spelling of the phoneme, either by writing a letter or letters into the box or by putting the appropriate tile or tiles in place. If they need to, students can subvocalize their segmentation as they fill each box. Each box represents one phoneme, but the grapheme for that phoneme may contain more than one letter. (For example, the *ch* sound in *witch* has three letters and the *a* sound in *eight* has four.)

- After writing in letters or putting down tiles, students should check their work by reading the sounds and then blending them together to make the target word.

- Finally, show the process to the students, saying the sounds and writing in the letters. The students should correct their word if it is not spelled incorrectly.

Figure 6.3 shows spelling grids completed by kindergarten and second-grade children. In the grids are the graphemes that represent the phonemes of *ship* and *rich*.

Figure 6.3 Kindergarten and second-grade spelling grids

Because I have been trained in Wilson Reading, I teach that some graphemes are made from letters "welded" together. A welded letter combination cannot be separated into its constituent parts. The nasalized *a* sound heard in *am* and *an* is an example of this, as is the "rounded" *a* sound heard in *all* and the "swallowed" *n* sound heard in *ng* and *nk* patterns such as *ank, ing, onk,* and *ung.* In these cases, the pattern itself dictates the sounds of the letters.

Figure 6.4 shows a "welded" letter group in the segmentation of *stamp.* The letter tiles are part of a Wilson Reading magnetic journal.

Elkonin boxes can be used in a variety of ways, and students in various stages of spelling development can use them. Young students in the sound-letter stage may use a three-box spelling grid to spell CVC and CVCC words such as *sip*, *bat*, *rich*, and *lock*. Older students or more advanced spellers might use the same three-box grid to spell *gaff*, *church*, and *thought*. Later, when students are adept at

Figure 6.4 "Welded" letter combination

segmenting and spelling sounds, give them one spelling grid five to seven boxes long. Then allow them to decide how many boxes they need to spell any given word. Reinforce to these students that, depending on the word given, they may not need to fill in every box. For example, the word *chin* fills just three boxes of a seven-block grid, *freight* fills four, and *unstrap* fills seven.

Word Ladders

Word ladders (also known as word-links, laddergrams, and doublets) involve transforming one word into another by changing one letter or set of letters at a time. Each change creates a new word, and each new word is a rung on the ladder. Starting with the word at the bottom of the ladder, it may take a speller five, six, or seven or more words to reach the target word at the top.

I first used word ladders while teaching in third-grade classrooms. Later I learned that Tim Rasinski made them popular with his Daily Word Ladders books for teachers (2008, 2012). But it was while doing research for this book that I discovered that Lewis Carroll was the one who invented them!

Carroll, best known as the author of *Alice's Adventures in Wonderland*, was also an eminent mathematician and a renowned puzzle creator. In 1877 he created a word puzzle that he dubbed the *doublet*, a name likely inspired by the witches' incantation in *Macbeth*: "Double, double, toil and trouble." *Vanity Fair* published Carroll's doublets in 1879, and they quickly became all the rage. Figure 6.5 lists five of his original doublets. It also shows a word ladder that can actually take you from one place to another! While visiting a botanical garden in New Zealand, my wife and I climbed these etched granite steps, took a picture from the top, and wrote the solution to the doublet in our scrapbook.

1. Turn POOR to RICH

2. Cover EYE with LID

3. Make WHEAT into BREAD

4. Change CAIN into ABEL

5. Evolve MAN from APE

Figure 6.5 Lewis Carroll's doublets and New Zealand word ladder

Like the Segment to Spell activity, word ladders help children notice sounds, especially inner vowels. To change one word into another, students must listen to sounds and decide on letters. Unlike Carroll, who gave puzzlers no clues about the ladder rungs, you can explicitly tell your students what each word on a rung is. Over time, as young children and struggling readers write each word in the ladder, they notice patterns within words and between words. If desired, you can also discuss the meaning of the words that make up a ladder. In this way, *spelling* becomes *vocabulary*!

There are plenty of word ladder activities available for purchase from Tim Rasinski and others. And I've included a few of Carroll's doublets (and their solutions), plus two of my own, in Appendix D of this book. But you can create the word sequences yourself. Figure 6.6 shows two word ladders I created: turn a PIG into a RIB and make a CHICK CHEEP. Although my ladders are in the spirit of Carroll's doublets, the words on either end of the ladder don't need to be tied together by a theme. Also, once students become accomplished at completing word ladders, you can put them to work making their own. It's a real accomplishment when a child authors a word ladder that becomes part of a literacy center.

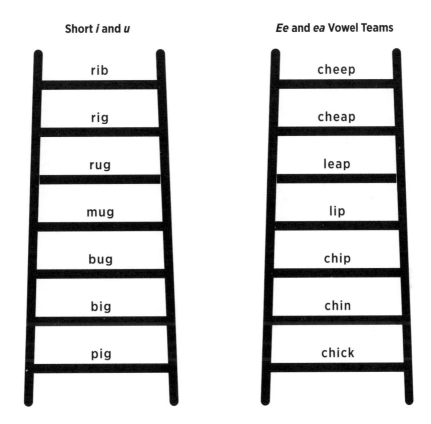

Figure 6.6 Teacher-created word ladders

I have used word ladder activities with large groups of kids, but I also have guided children through them in small groups during guided reading time, where I used a word ladder as a word study activity. Once children can competently re-create the routine on their own, they can complete word ladders with a buddy during independent work time.

You don't need a worksheet to do a word ladder. Simply have students write their sequences on paper. A whiteboard or iPad will work, but the written words need to be relatively small. Paper is probably best if your ladder is longer than five or six words. Students should never erase the previous word. The point is to create a sequence that students can look through to see the relationships between the words.

Let's say you created a word ladder that changes *pen* into *box* through this sequence: *pen, pet, pat, pit, sit, six, fix, fox, box*. To teach this word ladder, start with the word *pen*. Say the word and have the kids repeat it to you. You may even want to have the students stretch that word and zap it so they can hear the sounds in the word. I think highlighting inner vowel sounds is especially important, because I've found that these are the sounds hardest for students to hear, reproduce, and associate with correct letter combinations.

After students have written their starting word, you write the word and have your students check their spelling. Next, instruct students as follows:

> Change one letter in *pen* to make the word *pet*. Write the word *pet* above the word *pen*. [Pause while the students write. Then write *pet* above *pen,* modeling the segmenting of sounds, the writing of each letter, and rereading to check the word.]

> The letter we changed came at the end of a word. Now we are going to change a letter in the middle position. Change *pet* into *pat*. Let's stretch the word *pat* to hear the vowel sound. [Stretch the word with the students. Then repeat the steps of pausing while they write, modeling the correct spelling, and checking the word. Repeat the process for *pit, sit, six, fix, fox,* and *box*.]

Here is an example of what a teacher might say during a word ladder designed to focus on pattern and meaning, rather than just individual sounds and letters. The words come from the second of the two word ladders in Figure 6.6. After this teacher briefly reviews the *ee* and *ea* vowel teams, and after he or she has led the class through the first four words (*chick, chin, chip, lip*), the instruction might sound as follows:

> Change the vowel in *lip* to make the word *leap*. Write *leap* above the word *lip*. [Pause for student thinking and writing. Spell the word *leap*.]

> Now replace the beginning consonant with a digraph to make the word *cheap*. [Pause for student thinking and writing. Spell the word *cheap*.] The word *cheap, ch-e-a-p,* means inexpensive or doesn't cost much money. Now change the vowel team of this word to create a new word that sounds the same but has a different meaning. I want you to change *cheap* into *cheep*, the sound a chick makes. *"Cheep, cheep!"* [Pause for student thinking and writing.]

> How are *cheap* and *cheep* alike? How are they different? [Discuss with students.]

Once you start moving into this type of word ladder, Patricia Cunningham's Making Words books become a wonderful resource. There are probably a dozen or more of these books on the market, and they address many grade levels. Although not exactly word ladders, each lesson follows the basic process of swapping sounds and letters in and out of words to make new words. Each Making Word lesson draws on the letters of a relatively long target word, such as *oatmeal*, to create sets of smaller words that follow patterns, such as *eat, meat, team, meal, ate, mate, late,* and so on.

Word ladders and word-making activities are opportunities not only for children to hear sounds, assign letters, notice patterns, and think about meaning but also for you to conduct formative assessments. As you walk among the working students, notice who is confused about patterns or sounds and who is not. Explore their thinking process by saying, "Tell me why you put this letter here" and asking, "What pattern are you thinking about right now?" Carry a clipboard and piece of paper with you so you can take note of the children who require reteaching, as well as list the areas in which they need additional instruction.

Look Touch Say

I learned this quick and engaging routine during a LETRS (Language Essentials for Teachers of Reading and Spelling) training session. It's a nifty way to review letter sounds, syllable types, spelling patterns, word definitions, and much more. Because it constantly cycles back to the basics of what you want to teach, it promotes mastery learning, and because it takes only two to three minutes to complete, it makes for a good warm-up before word-building or word-dictation activities. I've modified and adapted it over time so I can use it in a variety of situations. Once you become familiar with it, I think you'll find yourself doing the same.

In our first scenario, we'll use Look Touch Say to teach common spelling patterns, and we'll use manipulatives rather than a word list as our material for teaching. To start, decide on the patterns you want to teach or review: word chunks such as *ate, ain, eep*, vowel teams (*ee, ai, oi*), r-controlled groupings (*or, ar, ir*), inflectional endings (*ing, er, ed*), and so on. Plastic tiles, magnetic tiles, foam blocks—anything will do. The materials I used with kindergartners and third graders came from companies such as Step by Step Learning, Touchphonics, and Wilson Language, but you can, of course, make your own materials.

Let's imagine it is November and you are teaching first grade. Let's also imagine you have been using the chart of thirty-seven high-frequency phonograms mentioned earlier as your scope and sequence. Your lesson last week focused on short-*o* families: *ock, op, ot*. This week your focus is the short-*u* families: *ug, ump, unk*. To reinforce the spelling of the patterns, as well as to have students notice the differences in the sound and spelling of the patterns, you decide to do five minutes of Look Touch Say. Here is a routine for the activity.

Have the students place the pattern tiles or blocks on their desks. Pick a pattern, such as *ump*, and say, "Look for *ump*." Follow that command with "Touch it." At this point, the students should be scanning only for the word part and then touching it with their index finger. Monitor their touches, and guide and correct anyone who has made an error. After two to five seconds, depending on the age and ability of your students, the number of manipulatives on their desks, and how much monitoring and correcting you are doing, give the command, "Say it!" At this point, the students should say the word part. After praising their attentiveness, go to the next pattern.

The routine is merely a repeated cycle of commands, which sounds like this:

Teacher: Look for *ock*. Touch it. [Pause.] Say it.

Students: *Ock*!

Teacher: Look for *unk*. Touch it. [Pause.] Say it.

Students: *Unk*!

Teacher: Look for *ump*. Touch it. [Pause.] Say it.

Students: *Ump*!

The Look For and Touch It commands give children think time. As you scan the room, wait until every child has found the word. Only then say, "Say it!"

You can mix in the command "Spell it" to create a routine that sounds like this:

Teacher: Look for *ock*. Touch it. [Pause.] Say it.

Students: *Ock*!

Teacher: Spell it.

Students: *O-c-k*!

Teacher: Look for *unk*. Touch it. [Pause.] Say it.

Students: *Unk*!

Teacher: Spell it.

Students: *U-n-k*!

Another variation is Look, Touch, See, Say, Spell. In this variation, you incorporate the all-important strategy of seeing the word (or in this case the pattern) in your head. But be careful: this sequence might be too much for young students.

Teacher: Look for *ock*. Touch it. [Pause.] See it. [Pause while students look at the pattern and then close their eyes.] Say it.

Students [Still with their eyes closed]: *Ock!*

Teacher: Spell it.

Students [Still with their eyes closed]: *O-c-k!*

You can also work in commands that are more open ended. For example, you might say, "Look for a pattern with the *u* sound." In this case, when you give the "Say it" command, some students might say *unk*, some might say *ug*, and some might say *ump*. This variation is not for teachers who like orderly responses, but if you're okay with a bit of chaos, try it out.

I have found that students learn the Look Touch Say routine quickly. Soon they will be ready to mimic you. When this is the case, ask for a volunteer to lead others, using a word he or she has picked.

Let's now consider doing Look Touch Say with a word list. First, pull a subset of words from your master list, print the subset as a list, and give the list to the large group or small group of students you are working with. It might look like Figure 6.7.

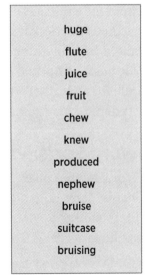

huge

flute

juice

fruit

chew

knew

produced

nephew

bruise

suitcase

bruising

Figure 6.7 Word list for Look Touch Say

Next, review the words by simply saying, "Look for *fruit*." Quickly follow that with "Touch it" and after a pause, "Say it." Next might be "Look for *nephew*. Touch it." [Pause.] "Say it." This type of direct and explicit review, cycled over and over again, can be especially helpful to ESL students who need practice and repetition in seeing and saying words.

Next, move to noticing patterns. For example, you might say, "Look for a word with the *ing* pattern. Touch it. Say it." Here all the children would say, "Bruising." But if you were to say, "Look for a word with the vowel-consonant-*e* pattern," then different children would touch and say different words. You might follow up their response with "Very good! I heard some say *huge*, some say *flute*, and others say *suitcase*. Those are all correct. Each has the vowel-consonant-*e* pattern."

Add a bit more by saying and asking the following: "Look at *huge* and *flute*. How are they alike? What long vowel sound is produced in those words? How is it spelled? Look at *suitcase*. Is that word similar to *huge* and *flute* in any way? How is it different? How many long vowel sounds are in that word? How are those sounds spelled?"

You can also think in terms of syllable types rather than patterns. For example, you might say, "I'm thinking of a word with an open syllable. Look." After the students look over their spelling list, say, "Touch." Students then touch a word with the appropriate syllable, in this case *produce*. Or you might say, "Look for a word with a vowel-consonant-*e* syllable," which leads to students pointing to and saying either *suitcase* or, more subtly, *produced*.

Finally, try bringing meaning into this routine. Start with a simple word definition routine, such as "Look for the word that means discolored skin that comes from an injury" (*bruise*) or "Look for a word that means the son of one's brother or sister" (*nephew*). Next, move to something more conceptual in nature, such as inflectional endings. A command for an inflectional ending might be "Look for a word that happened in the past. Touch it." [Pause.] "Say it." Here the students would respond, *"Produced."* This might be followed with a quick review of the inflectional ending, its meaning, and the principle for spelling it. This might be something like, "What spelling ending tells us an action happened in the past?" After the children respond with *"ed,"* you might say, "And what is our rule for adding an ending like *ed* to a word that already ends with *e*?" To this the students would respond, "Drop the *e* and add the ending."

Word Sorts: Patterns in Sound and Meaning

Word sorting plays an important role in spelling instruction. As students sort words, they notice their similarities and differences. This noticing increases their ability to fluently recognize and use a wide variety of patterns while spelling, writing, and reading. Word sorting helps students understand how patterns come together to create meaning, and it builds the mental word list that ultimately becomes the dictionary in their brain.

In general, I see the focus of any word sort as being either a sort for patterns that are sound based or a sort for patterns that are meaning based. Whether students are sorting for sound-based patterns or meaning-based patterns, it is critical that they explain their sorts. "Why?" "Why did you do that?" "Tell us why" and "Explain your sort to the class" are examples of language you can use when prompting students to make their thinking audible to others.

We'll tackle sound-based patterns first, and we'll do it using the eleven words listed in Figure 6.8.

Sort for Sound-Based Patterns

To do any type of sorting, words must be on cards. Some spelling programs come with word card blackline masters or even better, sets of printed cards. Printed cards have two big advantages: the work of putting words on cards is already done, and the words are spelled correctly every time. If you don't have printed cards, you'll have to create cards yourself or have your students make them. It's fine for students to copy spelling words onto cards, but if they do so, make sure their words are spelled correctly. If your students can master writing their words onto cards correctly, and if your routine calls for them to check their cards with a partner, then incorrect spellings on cards won't be an issue. But if the majority of your kids cannot copy correctly, then create the cards yourself.

wild

mild

kind

mind

child

pile

smile

sunshine

behind

wildlife

spellbinding

Figure 6.8 Words for a pattern sort

Begin your instruction by modeling a word sort. At this point you explicitly teach the pattern or patterns of the lesson. It's also the point where you demonstrate how one can be a pattern detective. Explain to your students that the goal of sorting is to notice similarities and differences and detect patterns. And don't forget to have a bit of fun! Wear a deerstalker hat, bring in a giant magnifying glass, and carefully inspect your cards for patterns.

If you were to use the words in Figure 6.8, here's what you might say during an initial lesson:

> Aha! I notice the words *wild* and *child* have the same pattern. Hmm . . . I see the vowel is closed in, but when I say the words, they make a long vowel sound, not a short one. Interesting! Now let me look at other words. *Smile* and *shine* have a vowel-consonant-*e* pattern. They make the same long *i* sound as *wild* and *child*. Hmm . . . I'm noticing that these other words, *kind* and *behind,* share the *ind* pattern. Now I'm making a

connection: *wild* and *child* are similar to *kind* and *behind* because they are all closed in at the end, yet they make the long *i* sound. Crazy!

To wrap up your introduction, model a word sort that places the words into three categories and explain why you did so. For example, you might explain Figure 6.9 by saying, "In this word sort I have placed the words *wild, mild,* and *child* into one category. They follow the *ild* pattern. The words *kind, mind, behind,* and *spellbinding* go into a second group because they all contain the *ind* pattern. Finally, *pile, smile,* and *sunshine* go into a third group. These words have the long *i* sound spelled vowel-consonant-*e*. *Wildlife* contains two patterns, *ild* and vowel-consonant-*e*. It can go into either category. Amazing!"

ild Pattern	*ind* Pattern	VCe
wild	kind	pile
mild	mind	smile
child	behind	sunshine
(wildlife)	spellbinding	(wildlife)

Figure 6.9 Three-category word sort based on sounds and patterns

Once you have modeled a sort to your class, give your students their own sets of cards, either individually or in pairs, and direct them through a closed sort (Figure 6.10). In a **closed sort**, you provide categories for sorting, saying, for example, "Sort your words by the sound patterns "*e* as in *Ed* and *o* as in *octopus*" or "Sort your words into two piles, one that contains compound words and one that contains all other words." Because a closed sort is typically teacher directed, there is little to no debate about where a word belongs. However, there may be opportunities for students to explain why they believe a word belongs in a different pile, so encourage discussion and thinking.

Figure 6.10 First-grade closed sort with word and picture cards

Open sorts, by contrast, are student directed and may be open to varied interpretations. Students decide on the categories for sorting, and there should be discussion about how and why specific words were grouped together. Your direction for an open sort might sound like this: "Look at your words. Notice how some words relate to one another. Put your words into two, three, or four groups. Make sure you have a reason for grouping words, and be prepared to tell everyone why you put certain words together."

Figure 6.11 shows two open sorts from two different students and the thinking behind each open sort for pattern.

wild	wildlife	pile
mild	sunshine	smile
child	spellbinding	
mind		
behind		
kind		

Student 1: "The first group has words that are closed-syllable rule breakers. The last group has words with a silent *e*. The middle group is compound words."

wild	wildlife	behind
mild		sunshine
child		spellbinding
pile		
smile		
kind		
mind		

Student 2: "The words in the first group have only one vowel sound. And they're all one syllable. *Wildlife* has only one vowel sound—long *i*—but it has two syllables. The words in the third group have more than one vowel sound in each word."

Figure 6.11 Open word sorts from two students

Clopen sort is a term I created because it's fun to say and, more importantly, because it provides a way to think about teacher-directed sorts that are somewhat specific, like a closed sort, but still open to interpretation, like an open sort. For example, using the words in Figure 6.8, you might say this about a clopen sort: "Sort the words by syllable types: closed, open, and vowel team. Some words might fall into more than one category, so decide where to put them and then be ready to explain why you put them there."

Here is an example of a clopen sort that isn't pattern based. Rather, it asks students to think about words used in writing: "Sort your words into two piles. In the first pile, put words that you might use frequently in writing. In the second pile, put words you won't use in writing very often." As in other clopen sorts, there is no wrong answer as long as the children can explain their thinking to you.

Independent sorts and buddy sorts

For additional practice, give your students the chance to sort their words on their own or with a partner. Word sorting can be done while others are finishing an activity, during morning work time, or even during whole-group practice time. After sorting words into two, three, or four categories, students can document the sort by writing it down. Not only does this provide accountability, but it also makes learning more permanent and builds pattern and word recognition fluency.

Secret sorts

Secret sorts are done with partners. The first student sorts the word cards into any number of piles but doesn't explain her criteria for sorting them. The second student then guesses the secret to her sort, or the criteria used for sorting. Another variation is a secret sort letter. One student writes her word sort on a letter, signs her name, folds the paper, and puts it in an envelope. She then puts the letter in another student's mailbox or places it in a "secret sort" tray. A second student opens the letter, solves the sort mystery, writes the secret (how the words were sorted), and then sends the letter back to the first.

Quick sorts

Kids love to do things fast, so harness that enthusiasm with quick sorts. The goal is to sort word cards into pattern-based categories as quickly as possible. Students can track their achievement with a timer though I'm of two minds here: timers make activities more fun and increase motivation, but they can also stress kids out or create too much competition. As always, do what you think your kids will benefit from most. If you allow them to use a timer, I'd encourage you to keep the focus on "achieving your personal best," not on besting others. You might want to have them keep a personal scorecard for recording sort times or pair up with a partner who will listen to the sorter explain how and why he or she sorted the cards, and operate the timer.

Closed, open, and clopen sorts from multiple lessons

Word cards from two or three lessons can be collected in zip-top baggies (I like the heavy-duty sandwich kind with a sliding zipper) and used for word sorts. Every student in the classroom can have a baggie, or baggies could be for buddy teams or in a literacy center. Including words from multiple lessons is a great way to review previously taught spelling concepts, broaden the scope of sorts, and build students' ability to think relationally. Just think of what closed, open, and clopen word sort directions you could give if your students had a baggie that contained all the words from the spelling lessons listed in Figure 6.12.

Lesson	Concept	Words
1	Long-*a* open syllable	paper, favor, lady, station, nation, baby
2	Long-*a* vowel team	rainy, claim, betray, playpen, strainer, trailer
3	Long-*i* vowel team	high, right, brighter, mighty, sighing, knight

Figure 6.12 Spelling lessons provide words for sorting

Word Sorts for Meaning-Based Patterns

Word sorts not only help students notice how patterns reflect the sounds of words, but can also help students understand how meaning is held within certain patterns. Word meaning arises from base words, root words, inflectional endings, and suffixes and prefixes. Many words are made from a Latin or Greek root plus an affix, so examining and discussing roots and affixes helps students build their vocabulary knowledge, increase their ability to read fluently and comprehend text, and, of course, spell more words correctly during writing.

The regular study of suffixes and prefixes typically begins in third grade, and instruction on Latin roots typically occurs in grades five and six. But if we think in terms of development and readiness, it's perfectly plausible that some students will be ready for meaning-based word parts at a younger age. Dr. Louisa Moats says that once prefixes and suffixes are recognized, "It's best to organize word study around a common root" (2005/2006, 12). So let's use a common Latin root, *ject* (to throw), and see what we can do with word sorts. Let's use the words in Figure 6.13.

When it comes to introductory teaching, I believe direct and explicit is best. I base this belief on research, the writing of spelling authorities such as Richard Gentry (2016a), and my many years of teaching children in special education and reading intervention classrooms. I'm pointing this out because some spelling authorities believe otherwise. Their belief is that constructive instruction should come first. In other words, they believe that children construct meaning through trial and error and exploration, that this type of learning is powerful, and that activities that support this type of learning should form the foundation of classroom instruction.

reject	Refuse to take; discard
eject	Expel; throw out
injection	Something that is put or shot into something else
dejected	Feeling sad; depressed; left out
project	1. A task; a thing to work on 2. Extend outward; protrude
projectile	An object shot or forcefully thrown into the air
subject	1. A thing to focus or concentrate on 2. Force upon; inflict upon
trajectory	The path of a flying object

Figure 6.13 Words for meaning-based word sorts

There is certainly research to support the "construction first" point of view. But there is also research to support the "direct and explicit first" point of view. If you choose to adopt my instructional viewpoint, then be direct and explicit about what spelling patterns to look for and what the words mean. For example, tell your students the focus of this week's lessons will be the Latin root *ject*. Say, "This week our focus will be the Latin root *ject*. What is the focus of our lesson, everyone? *Ject* means to throw. What does *ject* mean, everyone?"

When it comes to word meanings, rather than having students construct their own meanings or look up the words in a dictionary, provide them with short definitions via PowerPoint or on a Smartboard or blackboard. Make sure you translate dictionary language into kid-friendly language. (For examples of kid-friendly definitions, see Figure 6.13.) Then use language like the example below to teach the meaning of the word. I'll use the word *projectile*.

Teacher: The word is *projectile*. Say it.

Students: Projectile.

Teacher: A projectile is an object shot or forcefully thrown into the air. What is a projectile, everyone?

Students: An object shot or forcefully thrown into the air.

Teacher: The tornado turned tree branches into deadly projectiles. What does projectile mean in this sentence?

Students: The branches were objects thrown into the air. The tornado threw them into the air with force. [If the students don't know, quickly and directly supply the answer and have the students repeat it.]

Teacher: [Give a nonexample.] Is a floating feather a projectile?

Students: No. [If the students say yes, immediately and directly give the correct answer and have the students repeat it.]

Teacher: Why not?

Students: [Students should explain that a feather doesn't have force, isn't being thrown through the air, and so on.]

This direct and explicit routine is short, sweet, and powerful. Remember to keep your pace of instruction brisk. With repetition and practice, you'll be able to effectively introduce ten words in ten minutes or less.

Notice that I said *introduce*. To truly master the meaning and usage of a spelling word, students need many exposures to the word as well as time to thoroughly explore its meaning. Background knowledge, attention to the task, the ability to remember, and motivation to learn are just a few factors that affect the number of encounters a child needs in order to remember and understand a word. Because of these many variables, it's difficult to say definitively the number of repetitions that any student needs to learn a new word's meaning. Regardless of whether it is seven, twelve, or twenty, assume that your students need a lot! But no worries. You'll give them repetitions the next day, with a brief Look Touch Say routine, and the day after that, during a word sorting activity.

To explore meaning in a whole-group lesson, start with an open sort. Tell students to find two, three, or four words that relate to each other through meaning and to then group those words together. If students used the words in Figure 6.13, they'd surely group *project* and *projectile*. Others might group *eject*, *deject*, and *reject* because their first syllables (*e, re, de*) are open. Still others might group *eject*, *projectile*, and *trajectory* because when something is *ejected*, like a spitball from a straw, it becomes a *projectile* that travels along a *trajectory*.

Figure 6.14 gives another set of words to consider and shows how fourth graders sorted them. The words in each sort are the same, but the groupings are quite different. The kids who did the first sort told me they organized it by suffixes, with words ending in *ic, graphy,* and *logy* grouped together. The organizing principle for the second sort is Greek roots.

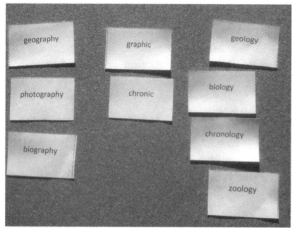

Figure 6.14 Fourth-grade word sorts for meaning

As in all sorts, your students should be explaining their thinking to you and to students around them. You can facilitate this explanation by regularly asking, "Why did you sort your words that way" or by saying, "Tell me why you sorted that way," "Tell me your thinking," "Explain your sort to your partner," and "Explain your sort to the class." Sorting and explaining makes invisible thought processes both visible and audible, which allows you to assess students' thinking. Equally important, it allows children to think divergently and take risks. There is no such thing as a wrong answer if a child can explain his or her thinking with reasons that make sense.

Later, move to a clopen sort. For example, you could tell students to create two categories, one for words that have to do with feeling sad and one for words that don't. If we go back to the *ject* words, *dejected* is an obvious choice for the first category. Other students might include the word *reject* because when you are rejected, you feel sad. Still others might include *subject*. As before, ask, "Why did you include that word in your sort?" If the student says, "Because when I'm *subjected* to lots of *rejection*, I feel sad and *dejected*," then you know this student has a firm grasp on word meaning.

Six-Word Storytelling

Direct and explicit instruction on the definitions of words, word definitions in kid-friendly language, and practice with word sorts for meaning all help students internalize the meanings of spelling words. Additional practice, which makes learning more perfect and permanent, can be provided with this storytelling activity. When students string together spelling words into sentences that tell a story, they build background and connections and practice relational thinking. Plus, telling a story is fun, especially when you give students time to share their stories with others.

When asking students to construct a story, ask them to use six words. You can challenge them to use more, but six is enough to create a story that is meaty but not too complex. Also, tell your students it's okay to add inflectional endings (*ing, ed, er*) to words. They can even add an affix or two. Here's a story constructed from the words in Figure 6.13:

> I went to a movie. There I saw images *projected* onto a giant screen. The movie was about a zoologist. He was *ejecting projectiles*, tranquilizer darts, from his gun, shooting at a lion. The *trajectory* of one of the darts was perfect. It hit the lion. Even though it was just drugged, I felt *dejected* when I saw the lion get shot. I began to sob. I bawled so loudly that an usher *ejected* me from the theater. Now I was mad. How dare they *subject* me to such humiliation?

Some students remember their stories best when they write them down. Others are capable of remembering their stories strictly from memory. Give your students options and everyone walks away happy.

Word Dictation

Word and sentence dictation give students the opportunity to listen, apply strategies, analyze mistakes, and think over the sounds, patterns, and meanings of words. This activity can be done in whole group, small group, or even with a buddy. The tools for writing can be old-school paper and pencil, individual whiteboards, or digital tablets. Figure 6.15 shows fourth graders writing teacher-dictated words on their iPads.

Finding words for dictation is easy; just look on your master spelling list. Keep the dictation session brief, maybe six or seven minutes, and allow a little time for discussion during the instant-error-correction phase of the activity. I'm

Figure 6.15 Students spelling dictated words

a big believer in both instant error correction and in the "I Do, We Do, You Do" instructional sequence. Here's an example of what this activity looks and sounds like when I teach it.

MW: Get your whiteboards and markers ready for writing, everyone. The word is *nephew*. Say it with me.

Students/MW: *Nephew.*

MW: You say it.

Students: *Nephew.*

MW: Listen: My nephew is eighteen years old. Write it.

Students: [They write on their whiteboards. As they write, I walk among them and scan for correct and incorrect words.]

MW: Listen: *nephew. N-e-p-h-e-w.* The *yoo* sound is spelled *e-w*. I see that everyone spelled that word correctly. You are really paying attention! Erase your boards [Students erase.] Get your markers ready for writing. The word is *cruising*. Say it with me.

Students/MW: *Cruising*.

MW: You say it.

Students: *Cruising*.

MW: Listen: I saw a shark cruising through the water. Write it.

Students: [They write on their whiteboards.]

MW: Listen: *cruising*. *C-r-u-i-s-i-n-g*. Everyone spelled the *oo* sound *u-i*. But I see some of you spelled the word *c-r-u-i-s-e-i-n-g*. Last month we learned that when adding *ing* to base words that end in *e*, we have to "drop the *e*, add *ing*." Let's repeat that.

All: "Drop the *e*, add *ing*."

MW: Watch. [I write *cruise*, erase the *e*, and then add *ing*.] If you misspelled this word, correct it right now.

When dictating unknown words, I use a little chant to reinforce the idea that words follow patterns and that a strategy for spelling is to use a known word to spell an unknown word (spelling by analogy). The chant is simply, "If you can spell _____, you can spell _____." Thus, when I ask children to spell the word *bruise*, I might say, "The next word is *bruise*. If you can spell *cruise*, you can spell *bruise*." Likewise, "The next spelling word is *bruising*. If you can spell *cruising*, you can spell *bruising*."

Sentence Dictation

In sentence dictation, students write a sentence that's completely decodable based on what they've previously learned in spelling. I began using this activity in heterogeneously grouped classrooms after I had done it for a year with my homogeneously grouped Wilson Reading intervention groups. I think it's an effective activity for two reasons. First, it gives kids the opportunity to apply spelling strategies across a string of words. Second, it asks children to listen closely to entire sentences and then remember what was said. I think you'll agree that listening and remembering is a skill many children (and adults) need to practice!

In April and May of 2016, I taught spelling for three weeks in a second-grade classroom. One of the weeks focused on two long vowel sounds: *i* spelled *i_e* and *u* spelled *u_e*. To help the students understand how adding a letter *e* to a CVC word can create a long vowel sound, I took the class through a sentence dictation activity. Figure 6.16 shows a child who has written dictated words and is now writing a dictated sentence. The words in each sentence came from my spelling master list, not from their take-home list. Because the students had never heard the words before, they had to apply sound and pattern knowledge to spell them, which is the point of using "unstudied" words.

I started the sentence dictation by saying, "I say a sentence, we say the sentence together, you say the sentence, and then you write the sentence. I say, we say, you say, you write! Get ready. Here's the sentence: *I spin the slim flute.* Say it with me: *I spin the slim flute.* Now you say it."

Figure 6.16 Word list based on a stand-alone program's word sort

Every student said the sentence—I could see every mouth moving—but I still wasn't sure they were all saying the right words. So I repeated the sentence one more time and had them repeat it. Next, after saying, "You write it," I walked through the class and monitored their progress. As students wrote, I noticed some of them pausing to repeat the sentence under their breath. I also noticed that almost all of the children were spelling the words correctly. Good for them!

Sentence dictation can take many forms. You can do it as a regular part of your spelling instruction or you can do it once or twice a month. You can have children write with paper and pencil, with whiteboard and marker, or with computer tablets and a writing program. You can incorporate the activity into your weekly spelling test. I used to offer it as an opportunity to earn a bonus point. Any student who spelled the entire sentence correctly and included correct capitalization and punctuation received a bonus point, which offset any misspelled word on a test.

If you feel the need to find sentences, programs such as Recipe for Reading, Wilson Language, and Step by Step Learning have them. Sentences can be made more memorable if they are goofy, and Step by Step Learning has word cards called Silly Sentence Cards. But I think you can make your own sentences. To create a sentence or two doesn't take much time, and with a little extra effort you can create ones that are amusing to elementary-age kids. Here are sentences using long-*u* words from the master list used in Chapter 4:

- *June was rude when she threw a cashew.*
- *When he sat on a juice box, my nephew bruised his butt.*

But why carry the burden of writing sentences on your shoulders? Put it on the kids! As Harry Wong would say to his students, "Get to work, get to work, get to work!" Challenge your students to craft silly sentences from their list of spelling words. After they submit them to you, look them over, reject any with incorrect mechanics, put the rest in a pile, and randomly draw two that will be read to the class during sentence dictation or for a spelling test bonus point. The children who are picked will be thrilled.

The trick is to come up with sentences created from spelling patterns that students have either learned to the point of mastery or are practicing in their current spelling lesson. So, if you teach kindergarten or first grade and are confident your students have mastered the sight words *my* and *his* (or if these words are on the word wall), and if your current focus is short vowel sound spellings (CVC words), then create sentences such as *Ted can nap on my bed* and *Sam had a bad rash on his leg.* If you teach fourth graders who have mastered closed and VC*e* syllables, and you are teaching open syllables, then create sentences such as *My dad demanded a refund, Will you retire?* and *I can't devote any time to the project.*

Strategy instruction, direct and explicit instruction, and practice before dictation increase student success during dictation, as does fostering an environment that is supportive of risk taking. Spelling unknown words and unpracticed sentences takes a certain amount of courage, because failure is always a possibility. But if students know it's okay to make mistakes, and if you praise them for hard work and effort, then they'll always be ready to try again.

Flip Folder

An easily constructed flip folder provides opportunities for students to practice the strategy "see the word in your head." The activity can be done independently or with a buddy. A flip folder is designed for instant error correction. A student spells a word and then checks it for correctness. If the word is misspelled, the student corrects it before moving on to the next word.

Flip folders are easy to construct. You'll need a manila folder, a marker, a set of word cards, and stack of blank slips of paper. The activity's routine mirrors the two-step word study strategy I outlined in Chapter 5: (1) Say-See, Hide-See, (2) Write, Check (and Correct). Here is a brief description of the routine, which is also shown in Figure 6.17.

- Students pick up a word card, say the word on the card, and visualize the word in their head. While teaching this step, encourage students to see the patterns in the words.

- Students lift the left flap and place the word card on the folder. They hide the word by putting the flap back down. Then they visualize the word in their head.

- Students pick up the right flap, put a blank slip of paper down, and write the spelling word. Then they lift the left flap and check to see if their spelling is correct. If the spelling isn't correct, they correct this error. (You'll notice in Figure 6.17 that the word is not spelled correctly and the student has not yet corrected her error.)

- Students remove both slips, set them aside, and start the process over.

Practice Test with Instant Error Correction

Giving a practice "test" with instant error correction is a simple yet effective way to promote mastery learning. Many students approach a test with a certain degree of gravity and attention. This is a good thing. But although this activity is called a test, it's really just a teaching activity. It's an especially effective one, however, because it makes use of immediate error correction.

Typically, practice tests are given so students know which words they need to practice for the "real" test. In some ways this is a good idea—students know where they stand and can take charge of their learning. But the teaching methodology typically employed in giving a test—giving all the words and then collecting the tests, correcting them, and handing them back at a later time—is somewhat to mostly ineffective. What's more, if the teacher, rather than collecting the tests at the end, has his or her students trade papers and correct them, then give them back to the original owner, the methodology is mostly a waste of time and even

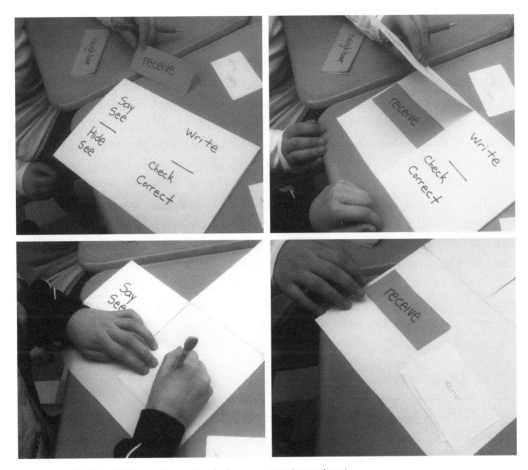

Figure 6.17 Word list based on a stand-alone program's word sort

a source of embarrassment. Numerous studies and reviews show that to be an effective instructional tool, feedback must be specific, immediate, goal directed, and free of competition (Hattie and Timperley 2007; Deci 2014; Samuels and Wu 2003). I don't often say, "Don't do this," but regarding the practice of having elementary-age students correct each other's tests, I must say, "Don't do this!"

When you give a test with instant error correction, you do *not* give the whole test and then go back and offer the correct spellings. Rather, you give correct spellings after each word. Why? Incorrect learning will not take root if it is immediately replaced with correct learning. Thus, student errors should be immediately addressed, explained, and corrected. Also, learning is stronger if students can immediately process what they've done right and what they've done wrong. All in all, instant error correction is a much more effective way to give a practice test. Here's what it looks like.

After having the students number their papers, say a spelling word, use it in a sentence, and then say it once more, just like you always do on a spelling test. Then immediately give the correct spelling by writing it on the board. As you say and spell the word on the board, have your students check their word. Anyone who misses a word should note where it is incorrect. Next, repeat the spelling of the word and have your students write this spelling next to their own spelling. Now they can see how their spelled word compares with your spelled word. If they made a mistake, they know where the mistake occurred and what type of mistake it is.

This routine is used for the entire test: teacher gives the word, students spell the word, teacher gives the correct spelling and students check, teacher spells the word again and students write it down, students check the first word against the second, teacher moves on to the next word. A time-tested, easy-to-learn, and easy-to-use technique for this type of checking is Dot and Circle. Figure 6.18 shows examples from second and fourth grade. As always, first model how the technique is done. Then have everyone practice.

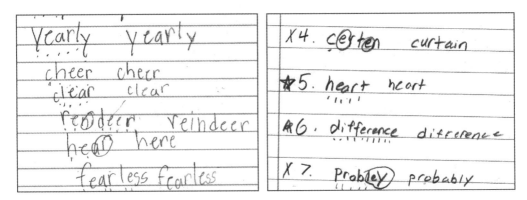

Figure 6.18 Dot and Circle for instant error correction

Here's how to teach the routine: After students write a spelling word, you spell the word letter by letter. As you spell, have your students place a small dot under each letter. Anyone who hears and sees a mistake in his or her word draws a circle in the area where the mistake or mistakes occurred. Don't allow students to erase. To compare, both words have to be intact. Next, spell the word one more time. As you spell, students spell the word correctly beside their initial spelling word. Finally, before moving on, give the class a few seconds to compare the two words. If you like, students who correctly spelled the first word can draw a star or smiley face next to it, or give a silent thumbs-up.

You needn't give all the words on a weekly list. If your class has a twelve-word list, give only six or seven words. If the class has twenty-four words, give only ten or twelve. And if you are running two lists, give six or seven words from each list to the appropriate group. Begin by having the students number their papers according to the number of words you will give. I'd suggest that you use a half-sheet cut horizontally (or what kids think of as a hamburger bun). This gives students enough vertical room to list ten or twelve words and enough horizontal room to write two words if needed.

As you give the test, meander among the students. Notice any spelling errors that occur frequently. If you notice that a number of children are having trouble with a particular sound, pattern, or meaning-part, I'd suggest that you immediately take thirty seconds and model how you thought about the correct spelling with a think-aloud. In other words, after the children have corrected their error, you model your thought process for using a spelling strategy by saying it out loud. For example, if you notice that seven out of twenty-four children spelled *passed* as *past*, you might say something like this:

> To spell this word correctly, I have to slow down and think about the meaning of the word in the sentence. When I hear someone say, "The driver *passed* me on the highway," I realize *passed* has to do with moving, like a quarterback throwing a pass or someone passing the salt. So I write the base word *pass*, and then I add my ending *ed*. I also remember that if *ed* is added to a word ending with the *s* sound, like *floss* or *miss*, the *ed* sounds like *t*.

Children are so habituated to seeing a spelling test as summative that you may have to reassure them, repeatedly, that it is okay if they miss a word or words because this is not a test that leads to a grade. You might also need to say that it is not cheating if they change (correct) their answers. The point of this test, which is formative, not summative, is threefold: (1) to give students information about what words they have mastered and what words they need to continue practicing, (2) to give you the same information, and (3) to put correct information into the brains of students sooner rather than later.

Once children grow accustomed to the routine of this type of practice test, they can give tests to each other in buddy groups during independent reading and writing time. Elementary-age kids love to do this because it gives one of the two buddies a chance to be the teacher for a few minutes. And what's better than being a teacher?

What's Next?

We are approaching the end of this book, but there's still a bit of work to be done. If we think of our transformed spelling instruction as a house, then the foundation and main rooms of assessment, strategy instruction, and teaching activities are finished. In the final chapter, we turn our attention to building a few last structures that will make our spelling house feel like a real home, where we are comfortable and confident about teaching and where the kids feel free and happy to learn. These finishing structures include opportunities for students to apply spelling skills in writing and in reading, with a bit of technology folded in.

IF YOU HAVE ONLY TEN MINUTES

- Go back to Figure 6.1, the initial list of spelling activities. Pick one of the activities and plan a lesson around it. Then teach that lesson. If you teach children, young or old, who need work in hearing the sounds of words and assigning the appropriate letters to them, then pick Segment to Spell or word ladders. If you have a majority of ESL students who need repeated practice in seeing and saying words, chose Look Touch Say. Teach word dictation or sentence dictation to students at any level.

- At the end of your first activity lesson, take five minutes to reflect on how the activity went. Did it work well? If yes, how can you create some momentum around the activity? If no, why didn't it work well? Do you and your students need to practice it more, or does a specific part of it not work well with your students? If the latter, can that part be modified? Jotting down a few notes in an "instruction journal" might help you the next time you roll out the activity.

EXPLORE CONNECTIONS

1. How do the activities presented in this chapter connect to what you learned in Chapter 1? How do they connect to what you learned in Chapter 2, specifically about formative assessment?

2. Pick a strategy from Chapter 5 and explore how the strategy connects to an activity given in this chapter. For example, does the strategy of hearing and spelling the sounds connect to Segment to Spell, to word card sorts, or to word dictation? If so, explain what the connections are.

3. Which activities would be best for making connections to your phonics program? If you teach in an upper grade that doesn't spend a lot of time on phonics, which strategy would be best suited for making connections to vocabulary or compreshension instruction.

CHAPTER 7

Build Opportunities

> **IN THIS CHAPTER**
>
> - We examine ways to connect spelling to reading, from presenting decodable sentences based on spelling patterns to building opportunities for students to read in as many places and in as many ways as possible.
>
> - We also discuss how to connect spelling to writing, especially in authentic writing situations. We will consider both old-school paper–and-pencil writing and digital forms, such as writing apps, online blogs, and web-based writing platforms.

Building Opportunities to Connect Spelling to Reading

Spelling is foundational to reading. We know that effective spelling instruction not only activates reading circuitry but also creates the neural pathways and cognitive "wiring" that lead to higher reading achievement. As the orthographic area of the brain gains importance, encoding and decoding develop. Soon patterns of all types are recognized and stored by the brain. Eventually words are saved in their entirety, ready for later use in reading and writing.

By now you should be familiar with the term *brain dictionary*. Student brains, and adult brains, too, activate this dictionary and draw upon it during fluent reading and writing. We can help students build their word repositories not only through stand-alone spelling lessons, but also by making direct, explicit, and repeated connections between spelling words and reading and writing them. Let's first look at ways of connecting spelling and reading.

Reading Decodable Sentences

The focus of this book is encoding. But because decoding is the flip side of encoding, it makes sense for us to give our students opportunities to read highly decodable sentences. This is especially true for younger students who are learning how to read and for older students who are struggling to master sound-letter relationships and patterns. To make your instruction as effective as possible, phonics and spelling lessons should walk hand in hand.

When it comes to practicing phonics, one option is to have students read *instructional*-level decodable sentences, either with the whole group or with small groups during guided reading or intervention lessons. Instructional-level sentences contain words made from spelling features currently being studied. Thus, if your current spelling list includes the ending *ure* (*pressure, fissure, disfigure, nature, rapture*), appropriate sentences for reading would be "A cat's nature is to catch mice," "A fissure in the ice opened up," and "Don't pressure me to eat sardines." The reading of decodable sentences can also be done before a spelling activity. Either way, it's important to directly and explicitly show that the patterns in the sentence words are the same as the patterns being studied in the spelling words.

Another reading option is to have students read sentences with previously studied phonics/spelling patterns during *independent* reading time. List decodable sentences explicitly or, more flexibly, make them part of the reading center that's listed on your "I Can . . ." list (see Figure 7.1). If you give kids tools like whisper phones, witchy-poo fingers for finger tracking, and paintbrushes for paintbrush reading ("read like a painter, not like a pointer"), you will make repeated practice more engaging (see Figure 7.2 for examples of these tools). The goal is to motivate kids to practice. It's only through practice that students become fluent readers with an appropriate rate of speed, a high degree of accuracy, and pleasing expression and phrasing.

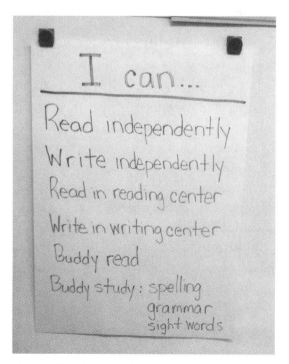

Figure 7.1 I Can list with reading center option

Figure 7.2 Ways to make repeated practice engaging

Reading decodable sentences is an opportunity for students to practice the sound, letter, and meaning patterns they are practicing in spelling now or have practiced in the past. You need to devote only five to seven minutes to this type of reading, but I suggest you program it regularly throughout the week, month, and year, especially for your struggling readers.

Decodable sentences can be found in programs such as Wilson Language, Recipe for Reading, and Step By Step Learning, and newer versions of basal programs often have decodable sentences as part of their phonic or intervention components. You can also make your own sentences. Pull words from your spelling lesson, put them into sentences, type the sentences on a sheet, and put the sheet in your reading center. Or have your kids write sentences and submit them to you. Look them over, pick the best ones, type them up, and make a book or binder that can go into a center.

Remember that no matter where the sentences come from, they should be made of words created from spelling patterns that students have either learned to the point of mastery or are practicing in their current spelling lesson.

Going on Word Hunts and Scavenger Hunts

Kids everywhere love to go hunting and scavenging. Apply this idea to finding words in a book and you'll have an engaged group of students. Start with text that has been previously read. For example, ask your students to choose a favorite book, story, or article they've read this week. Then send them on a word hunt. They can find words that match the spelling focus of the week, or scavenge for sounds, patterns, and meaning parts from previous lessons. Like the reading of decodable sentences, you need to devote only five to seven minutes to this type of activity. Here are options for conducting word hunts and scavenger hunts (with lists):

- During shared reading time, ask your entire group to search their current story for words that use the spelling focus of the week. The search could be for a letter-sound relationship ("Look for words that begin or end with *sh* or *ch*"), a pattern ("Look for words that contain *ief, ield,* or *eigh* patterns"), or a word part that holds meaning ("Look for words that contain a prefix," "Look for a word that has a Latin root," or "Look for a word with an ending that signals past tense"). If you keep the duration of the search short but provide multiple sessions, you will have given your students *distributed repeated practice*, an especially effective instructional technique (Benjamin and Tullis 2010).

- Do the activity during a guided reading lesson, the perfect place to work in some differentiated instruction. For example, two of your groups might look for single-syllable words that use the vowel-consonant-*e* syllable, while another group might look for multisyllabic words containing a combination of syllable types.

- Put "Word Hunt" on your I Can list or make it part of your reading center. Give your students the goal of searching for words that follow the spelling pattern of the week (such as the *ph* and *wh* digraphs, the *igh* and *i_e* patterns, or the Latin root *ject*). If students choose to work independently, they can pick any independent reading book. If they choose to work with a buddy, they can choose two different books or they can choose multiple copies of the same book. Up the accountability by requiring students to jot down the book title and list their words on a piece of paper (Figure 7.3).

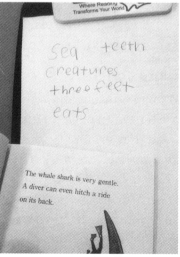

Figure 7.3 Second graders on a word hunt

- Put "Scavenger Hunt" on your I Can chart or make it part of your reading center. To create a scavenger hunt, provide your students with a form that lists the type of words you want them to find (see Figure 7.4). When they find the word, they check it off the list, write the word or words they've found, and give the page number on which they found it. A scavenger hunt is an engaging way to review previously studied spelling features. If you teach younger students, limit the number of features students look for. But if you teach older kids, give your students six or seven categories of words to find. Like most activities in school, a scavenger hunt is more fun (and engaging) if it's done with a buddy.

Figure 7.4 Form for a scavenger hunt

Scavenger Hunt		
Hunt completed by _H + Z_ on _1/12_		
Book or books used _Stone Fox_		

Search for	Word or words	Page #
Two words with patterns that make a long O sound		
Two words that begin with a prefix		
Three words that end with a suffix	question examanation official	
Three two-syllable words	harvest	
Four three-syllable word	grandfather excitement	
Two words with an open syllable		

Read, Read, Read

Reading theory tells us that the more children read, the greater chance they have of improving their fluency, building their background knowledge, and increasing their vocabulary. When kids read greater amounts of text, they increase the chance that they will commit whole words to their brain dictionaries, thus becoming better spellers, too. So it makes great sense for all of us to increase, as much as possible, the breadth and depth of the reading that takes place in our classrooms. In other words, make room for reading!

For teachers who work in a classroom based on balanced literacy or reading workshop, making room for reading is typically not a problem. Engaging students for extended amounts of time in a wide variety of independent and instructional-level texts is a pillar of these frameworks. But for teachers working with basal programs, the task is more difficult. In my book *Super Core* (Weakland 2014), I explore how to minimize and even eliminate basal components to make time for extended reading and writing. Throughout that book, I suggest that basal-using teachers minimize summative testing, deemphasize the anthology stories and the activities that surround them, deemphasize grammar that has little to do with writing expectations, and throw out as many worksheets and workbooks as possible. Doing this maximizes the amount of time students engage in authentic reading and writing tasks.

Now more than ever, teachers have options for giving students a wide variety of reading material on their independent and instructional levels. Kids can read digitally on Kindles, on iPads, and online. Options for printed reading material include magazines, graphic novels, manga, books from a classroom library, books from a school library, leveled books from a book room, binders of student-created writing . . . The list goes on. When students read, read, read, they increase their chances of becoming competent readers, writers, and spellers. It's a win-win-win situation. What can be better than that?

Building Opportunities to Connect Spelling to Writing

In Chapter 1, I proposed that although spelling should be taught as a stand-alone subject, it should also be directly and explicitly linked to reading and writing. Writing widely, like reading widely, exposes students to more words and provides better background knowledge of how commonly used words are spelled. When children write, they think about spelling. They see words over and over again as they revise and read their writing, and as they share their writing with multiple audiences (a buddy, the classroom, a parent). So the question becomes, how can you program more writing opportunities into your teaching day, especially ones that are authentic, engaging, and enjoyable?

Process Writing

Writing workshop, process writing, authentic writing—no matter the name, this type of writing increases the chance that your students will see writing as a meaningful and enjoyable activity. When kids enjoy writing and see it as a meaningful thing to do, they are much more likely to want to write. Eagerness to write leads to more writing, which leads to greater writing ability (fluency, command of language, command of grammar, and so on). In turn, increased ability can lead to higher achievement on longer written responses and essays. Ideally, all this writing will generalize to an increased ability to write for real-world reasons later in life. But more immediately, writing gives students opportunities to practice spelling based on sound, pattern, and meaning, as well as opportunities to put scores of words into their brain dictionaries.

Making room for extended writing is easier for teachers working within balanced literacy or reading workshop frameworks. Conversely, programming time for extended writing can be more difficult for teachers working with basal programs. The reasons are many. Basal programs suck up valuable instructional time with worksheets and analytical writing tasks (open-ended questions, text-dependent analysis prompts, and the like). When children spend too little time writing to express thoughts, interests, and ideas, they come to see writing as a chore. And who wants to do chores?

At a recent workshop, I presented the following as a way for teachers to think about their writing time. Regardless of how many minutes they had for writing every week, I suggested they devote

- 30 percent of their time to analytical writing—that is, writing to open-ended questions, writing to text-dependent analysis prompts, and so on;

- 30 percent of their time to prompt-based narrative, informational/explanatory, and opinion/persuasive/argumentative writing; and

- 40 percent of their time to authentic process writing (writing workshop, writing with choice, extended time to practice, conferencing, and sharing).

Educator and author Rose Cappelli, who was in the audience, suggested in a personal communication that the list be inverted, with the process writing coming first. "Structures such as writing workshop support the process of writing. Writer's workshop is where a love of writing and a community of writers is built," she said. "Once that's established, the rest of the writing will flow" (2016).

I couldn't agree more. If you increase the amount of time kids spend writing about authentic topics, if you give them choice, and if you provide opportunities for them to share what they have written, then you will increase both their love of writing and their writing competency. The leap of faith occurs when you believe that they will then approach prompt writing and test writing with less resistance and greater skill.

If you are a teacher unfamiliar with writing workshop, pick up a copy of *Writing Workshop: The Essential Guide* (Fletcher and Portalupi 2001). Or go to the writing chapter in my book *Super Core*, where I explain how a teacher who uses a basal reading program can carve out time to implement a "modified Writer's Workshop." In a perfect world, students would be writing every day without interruption for twenty to thirty minutes or more as part of a forty- or fifty-minute writing workshop session. But in your room, the reality might be two thirty-five-minute sessions of process writing a week. Even if you devote this amount of time, your students will begin to see writing as an enjoyable activity, not a dreaded task, and they will have more opportunities to practice their spelling and store words in their brains.

If your district is fortunate enough to have computers or electronic tablets that are regularly and easily accessible to students, then by all means, have your kids write for extended amounts of time on web-based writing platforms or hardware-based apps. Technology motivates, so if you have it, use it. There are many digital platforms conducive to student writing.

Scrawlar (scrawlar.com) provides cloud-based word processing. To start, create an account for your class and then add students to your network. Because Scrawler is web based, there is no app, no plug-in, and no installation required. And because it's cloud based, it's accessible to students at home. Powered by a simple text editor, the site allows students to integrate images into their work, supports collaboration and sharing among writers, and gives you the ability to provide feedback in real time.

Another platform to consider is Draft (draftin.com). Like Scrawler, Draft allows kids to integrate images into the text, and like Google Docs, it has a collaborative feature that allows multiple writers to work on the same piece of writing. Writers can also leave feedback for one another. "Hemingway Mode" is a feature that, when activated, turns off the writer's ability to delete. This means you can't go back and edit or revise! You can only continue writing forward. Later, when all your thoughts are safely saved, you can go back, turn off the feature, and revise your work.

Story Bird (storybird.com) is a writing platform that also functions as an e-book library. It's free for any educational setting, and it works with any device. Story Bird uses illustrations to inspire students to write stories, such as picture books for younger kids and chapter books for older students. The site also promotes the writing of poetry and blogs. Because the site functions as a library, students can publish their works as well as read the writing of others.

Like Story Bird, Widbook (widbook.com) is a free writing platform where writers can publish their own e-books. It allows multiple students to work on a project, and it has a chat feature so that writers can discuss edits and revisions while working. It also supports writers importing pictures, text, links, and videos into their writing.

Write the World (writetheworld.com) bills itself as an online community for writers. You can use the platform to create a private writing group for an individual class or grade level, and establish yourself (or a colleague) as a group manager who mentors students through the writing process. Additionally, the site provides students with its own writing prompts, as well as writing competitions. These features give students encouragement and ideas, which are crucial supports for many student writers.

Finally, you can explore blogs as a way for your students to express themselves in writing. A good place to begin is Edublogs (edublogs.org). Powered by WordPress, the site currently claims that it has hosted more than three million blogs since 2005. It offers many teacher-friendly features, such as video embedding, calendars, and discussion tools, as well as more than 100 themes that students can use to customize their blog.

Weebly (weebly.com) is another blog option. Best known as a builder of websites, the company offers teachers up to forty free student accounts (no e-mails necessary) that can be used for blogging. The blogs are ad-free, can be built from more than seventy different templates using a simple drag-and-drop interface, and can accept uploaded pictures and videos. Teachers have the ability to manage student blogs, which can be kept private or made public. In the interest of full disclosure, my website (MarkWeaklandLiteracy.com) is powered by Weebly, and I think it offers a great product.

Many digital writing platforms come equipped with a spell-checking tool. As with any tool, children must be taught how to use it. A spell-checker provides a writer with an opportunity to "take action." Thus, the responsibility is on the writer to try to correct the misspelled word to the point where the spell-checker can give a viable alternative. This may take a number of tries, which may involve a number of strategies (hearing the sounds of the word, thinking of an analogous word, and so on). I also suggest that you encourage your students to keep writing, rather than stop and attempt a spelling correction right then and there. Like the circle of the "circle the word and correct" strategy, a squiggly red line under a misspelled word says "pay attention." But writing doesn't have to come to a screeching halt. Rather, a writer can go back and correct for spelling errors once his or her thoughts are firmly in place.

Finally, you may have to explicitly and directly teach your students how to approach the words a spell-checker presents. Students can be too accepting of a spell-checker's word offerings, clicking on the first one that pops up and not reading it carefully to check for meaning. We've all had experiences like my colleague's sixth grader who, while preparing a social studies presentation, had a spell-checker insert "Greek orthodontics" when he really wanted "Greek Orthodox."

Draft, Story Bird, EduBlogs, Weebly—their use depends upon your access to technology as well as your students' ability to type. Last year, while working alongside dozens of teachers in nine different elementary schools, I noticed that writing technology was mostly absent from the classrooms. When I asked, "Why no technology?" I was told that because there were few keyboarding classes, and because students don't typically type at home, keyboarding skills were sorely lacking. Thus, it was much faster for students to write with a pencil on paper. Besides, old-school pencil-and-paper writing is how more than a few famous authors write. What's good enough for Neil Gaiman and Joyce Carol Oates is good enough for fourth and fifth graders!

Write, Write, Write

Wherever and however your students write, remind them that practice makes perfect and permanent. If students are to become competent writers, they need to practice more than just authentic writing. They'll also need to practice analytical writing, writing in response to reading, writing to summarize concepts, and writing to explain their mathematical thinking.

If you follow Rose Capelli's advice and start your students on writing workshop at the beginning of the year, then later in the year, perhaps in mid-November, you can begin to bump up the amount of time you devote to analytical writing. Perhaps you'll teach your students the RACE strategy (Restate, Answer, Cite, Explain) and have them practice answering text-dependent questions. Then in January, maybe you'll bump up the number of writing prompts you give or launch into lessons on writing literary essays (à la Lucy Calkins).

All this writing gives students opportunities to practice spelling to the point of perfection and permanency. This is especially true if you aid the process by reminding students to practice their spelling strategies, such as zap by sound, spell by analogy, think about meaning, and circle the word and come back. The human brain is a pattern-recognition machine, and writing gives recognition a chance to increase. In turn, recognition provides the foundation for remembrance.

IF YOU HAVE ONLY TEN MINUTES

- At the end of a shared reading with your classroom, take five minutes to send the children on a word hunt. Put two to four spelling patterns on the board, have your kids partner up, and then have them write down the words they find that follow the patterns. As they write, monitor them and guide them to correct any errors. Take an additional two or three minutes to "whip around" the room, having the partners say, spell, and say again one of the words they found. Or give two sets of partners two minutes to share their words with each other.

- If you have technology in your classroom in the form of tablets and/or computers, take ten minutes this week and explore the Story Bird (storybird.com) and Widbook (widbook.com) websites. Next week take another ten minutes to explore the Scrawler (scrawler.com) and Draft (Draftin.com) writing platforms. Finally, sketch out a writing project that would allow you and your class to explore writing through one of these online platforms.

- If you don't have a leveled classroom library, commit to spending ten minutes a week to level some percentage of your library. Start by sorting some chunk of the library into three boxes—clearly below grade level, on or near grade level, and clearly above grade level. Spend ten minutes a week for six or eight weeks until your library is leveled. Finally, commit to giving your students fifteen minutes of extended reading two times a week. During this time, students can choose books from any appropriate bin (or bring out a favorite book from home or the school library) and then read, read, read!

EXPLORE CONNECTIONS

1. What are the general connections among spelling, reading, and writing?

2. What is the specific connection between phonics and spelling words? How might you go about connecting the two more explicitly in your classroom instruction?

3. How can you generally and specifically weave instruction on spelling strategies into your writing lessons?

4. Having read this book up to this point, what would you write as an epilogue?

Epilogue

It is time to end our journey through spelling instruction. I'd like to wrap up with a few thoughts on literacy theory, instructional practice, and the importance of you, the teacher.

This book is about transforming ineffective spelling instruction, strengthening instruction that is already working but could be better, and using spelling as a way to develop reading and writing skills. Throughout, we've looked at spelling instruction in two ways: through the narrow lens of spelling development and through the wider lens of reading and writing development. As we learned way back in Chapter 1 (see Figure 1.3), the layers of literacy development—reading, writing, and spelling—are concurrent and interrelated. Thus, one of this book's main points is that excellent spelling instruction is a necessary part of a holistic literacy program. Another point is that excellent spelling instruction is critical to students who struggle to master key components of reading and writing.

We know that spelling is important because researchers of all types, from linguists to neuroscientists, have uncovered the facts about how spelling (and reading and writing) work within the brain and are constructed by the mind. These facts come together and show how literacy arises. In other words, the facts support a theory.

In science, the word *theory* is not synonymous with the word *belief*. One definition of *belief* is "confident thinking not necessarily supported by facts." A scientific theory is something very different. To paraphrase scientists Kenneth R. Miller and Peter Godfrey-Smith (as cited in Zimmer 2016), a theory is a network of explanations that ties together a large group of facts. It's like a map, representing a territory of science.

I love this analogy. Facts are to a theory as features are to a map. Likewise, a geography map is to a territory of earth as a theory map is to a territory of science. The best maps—derived from decades of observation, experimental confirmation, and replication—are highly descriptive and strongly predictive. Thus, they are tremendously useful. Well-established maps provide paths of action, enabling us to solve problems, alleviate suffering, and plan for the future.

We are fortunate to have strongly predictive maps at our disposal. Reading is probably the most extensively and intensively studied subject in the field of education. Instruction is also rigorously studied, and a theory of instruction (a map) is increasingly realized. We know, among other things, that instruction should be direct and explicit at times, that positive reinforcement molds behavior, and that providing feedback (during writing and reading and spelling) leads to greater learning.

As you move forward with your teaching, I encourage you to use the map of spelling instruction. It has been constructed over the decades through the great effort of many dedicated researchers. The features of this map, which I have done my best to describe in this book, include but are not limited to

- the developmental stages of spelling;

- the knowledge that spelling is for reading;

- the use of formative assessment to inform instruction and the use of spelling inventories to create groupings for differentiation and to track growth;

- the understanding that sound, pattern, and meaning are the basis for spelling lessons; and

- the spelling strategies that teachers can teach and students can use, such as hearing and spelling sounds, using known words to spell unknown words, creating and using mnemonics, seeing a word inside your head, and approximating a spelling and then circling it for later correction.

But the map of spelling theory is of no value unless you use it and use it well. To continue the map analogy, you are your students' guide across the literacy landscape, and if your students are to reach the destinations of reading, writing, and spelling success, then you must not only have an excellent map, but also be a skillful leader. As researchers such as John Hattie, Raj Chetty, and others have shown time and time again, when looking at school-based factors that affect student learning, teachers matter the most (Chetty et al. 2011; Hattie 2003). Your expertise is critically important, because in a school setting, the teacher is the number one agent of change for students.

Knowing this, knowing that it's *you* who matters most, may be a source of stress. And although some people thrive on stress, most do not. I know I don't!

So even as I encourage you to become a spelling expert, to transform "stuck" spelling instruction, to implement best practices, and to become a skillful and knowledgeable guide, I also encourage you to relax as much as possible and remember that there can be great joy in teaching. It's a matter of striking a balance. Not too loose, but not too tight.

Becoming a master teacher is a goal worth pursuing because masterful teaching leads to great amounts of student learning. And so I wish you the best in your teaching endeavors. I know you will do well! Outfitted with the information in this book, as well as your curiosity, experience, and expertise, you have all the tools you need to engage in spelling instruction that teaches students how to spell, write, and read.

Primary Short-Form Spelling Inventory for a Class

Date _____   Teacher Name _____

Word	Spelling Features	Highlight spelling features that more than 20% of class missed.
Set	s-e-t	
Mob	m-o-b	
Dip	d-i-p	
Hug	h-u-g	
Flash	fl-a-sh	*Beginning consonants
Slick	sl-i-ck	*Middle consonants
Hill	h-i-ll	*Ending consonants
Mess	m-e-ss	*Beginning blends
Junk	j-u-nk	*Beginning digraphs
Bottle	b-o-tt-le	*Ending digraphs
Stone	s-t-one	*Soft *c*
Grapes	gr-ape-s	*nk*
Chime	ch-ime	*Doubled consonant (*tt*)
Flute	fl-ute	
Faithful	f-ai-th-ful	*Short vowel sounds
Dream	dr-ea-m	*v_e* vowels
Coach	c-oa-ch	*Other long vowels (*igh, ea, oa*)
Lightest	l-igh-t-est	*Variant vowels (*oi, aw*)
Coin	c-oi-n	
Sprawl	s-p-r-aw-l	*Suffixes (*y, ful*)
Yard	y-ar-d	*Final syllables (*le*)
Thorny	th-or-n-y	*Endings (*s, es, ed, ing*)
Burned	b-ur-n-ed	
Shirt	sh-ir-t	
Wishes	w-i-sh-es	
Snapped	s-n-a-pp-ed	
Hiding	h-i-d(e)-ing	
Racing	r-a-c(e)-ing	

Primary Short-Form Spelling Inventory for an Individual

Date _____   Student Name _____

Word	Spelling Features	Highlight feature if student missed two or more.
Set	s-e-t	
Mob	m-o-b	
Dip	d-i-p	
Hug	h-u-g	
Flash	fl-a-sh	*Beginning consonants
Slick	sl-i-ck	*Middle consonants
Hill	h-i-ll	*Ending consonants
Mess	m-e-ss	*Beginning blends
Junk	j-u-nk	
Bottle	b-o-tt-le	*Beginning digraphs
Stone	s-t-one	*Ending digraphs
Grapes	gr-ape-s	*Soft *c*
Chime	ch-ime	*nk
Flute	fl-ute	*Doubled consonant (*tt*)
Faithful	f-ai-th-ful	
Dream	dr-ea-m	*Short vowel sounds
Coach	c-oa-ch	*v_e vowels
Lightest	l-igh-t-est	*Other long vowels (*igh, ea, oa*)
Coin	c-oi-n	
Sprawl	s-p-r-aw-l	*Variant vowels (*oi, aw*)
Yard	y-ar-d	
Thorny	th-or-n-y	*Suffixes (*y, ful*)
Burned	b-ur-n-ed	*Final syllables (*le*)
Shirt	sh-ir-t	*Endings (*s, es, ed, ing*)
Wishes	w-i-sh-es	
Snapped	s-n-a-pp-ed	
Hiding	h-i-d(e)-ing	
Racing	r-a-c(e)-ing	

Intermediate Short-Form Spelling Inventory for a Class

Date _____   Teacher Name _____

Word	Spelling Features	Highlight spelling features that more than 20% of class missed.
Lunch	l-u-n-ch	
Mesh	m-e-sh	*Beginning consonants
Thistle	th-i-st-le	*Middle consonants
Wrack	wr-a-ck	*Ending consonants
Botched	b-o-tch-ed	*Beginning digraphs
Trampled	tr-a-mp-l(e)-ed	*Ending digraphs
Hungry	h-u-ng-r-y	*Silent letters (*wr, t*)
Battle	b-a-tt-le	*Soft *c*
Pennies	pe-nn-i-es	*ng
Strove	str-ove	*Doubled consonant (*tt, nn, pp*)
Place	pl-ace	*dge
While	wh-ile	*voiced *s*
Tulips	tu-lip-s	
Flavoring	fla-v-or-ing	*Short vowel sounds
Lightest	l-igh-t-est	*v_e vowels (*ove, ace, ile*)
Spoiler	sp-oi-l-er	*Open syllables (*tu, fla*)
Groom	gr-oo-m	*Other long vowels (*igh*)
Drawn	dr-aw-n	*Variant vowels (*oi, oo, aw*)
Deserving	de-serv-ing	*Schwa *a*
Abnormal	ab-norm-al	
Awareness	a-w-are-ness	*Prefixes (*in, dis, con, pre*)
Confusion	con-fus-ion	*Suffixes (*ness, ion, ible*)
Invisible	in-vis-ible	*Latin roots (*fus, vis, quo, judg*)
Disappearance	dis-a-pp-ear-ance	*Final syllables (*_le, ure, al*)
Quotient	quot-i-ent	*Endings (*s, ed, ing*)
Prejudge	pre-judge	
Pleasure	pleas-ure	
Naturally	nat-ur-al-ly	

Intermediate Short-Form Spelling Inventory for an Individual

Date _____   Student name _____

Word	Spelling Features	Highlight feature if student missed two or more.
Lunch	l-u-n-ch	
Mesh	m-e-sh	*Beginning consonants
Thistle	th-i-st-le	*Middle consonants
Wrack	wr-a-ck	*Ending consonants
Botched	b-o-tch-ed	*Beginning digraphs
Trampled	tr-a-mp-l(e)-ed	*Ending digraphs
Hungry	h-u-ng-r-y	*Silent letters (*wr, t*)
Battle	b-a-tt-le	*Soft *c*
Pennies	pe-nn-i-es	
Strove	str-ove	*ng*
Place	pl-ace	*Doubled consonant (*tt, nn, pp*)
While	wh-ile	*dge*
Tulips	tu-lip-s	*voiced *s*
Flavoring	fla-v-or-ing	
Lightest	l-igh-t-est	*Short vowel sounds
Spoiler	sp-oi-l-er	*v_e* vowels (*ove, ace, ile*)
Groom	gr-oo-m	*Open syllables (*tu, fla*)
Drawn	dr-aw-n	*Other long vowels (*igh*)
Deserving	de-serv-ing	*Variant vowels (*oi, oo, aw*)
Abnormal	ab-norm-al	*Schwa *a*
Awareness	a-w-are-ness	
Confusion	con-fus-ion	*Prefixes (*in, dis, con, pre*)
Invisible	in-vis-ible	*Suffixes (*ness, ion, ible*)
Disappearance	dis-a-pp-ear-ance	*Latin roots (*fus, vis, quo, judg*)
Quotient	quot-i-ent	*Final syllables (c-*le, ure, al*)
Prejudge	pre-judge	*Endings (*s, ed, ing*)
Pleasure	pleas-ure	
Naturally	nat-ur-al-ly	

Primary Long-Form Spelling Inventory

Basic Syllable Type	Spell Stage → Word	Letter Name—Alphabetic Principle (Earlier Later)					Patterns Within Words			Syllables	
		Consonants			Short Vowel	Consonant Digraph	Consonant Blends	Long Vowel	Other Vowel	Final	Inflected Endings
		Begin	Mid	End							
Closed	1. set	s		t	e						
	2. mob	m		b	o						
	3. dip	d		p	i						
	4. hug	h		g	u						
	5. flash				a	sh	fl				
	6. slick					ck	sl				
	7. hill			ll							
	8. mess			ss							
	9. junk	j					nk				
	10. bottle		t							tle	
VCe	11. stone							o-e			
	12. grapes						gr	a-e			s
	13. chime					ch		i-e			
	14. flute							u-e			
Vowel Team	15. faithful		f			th		ai		ful	
	16. dream						dr	ea			
	17. coach							oa			
	18. lightest		t					igh			est
R-control	19. coin								oi		
	20. sprawl								aw		
	21. yard								ar		
	22. thorny								or	y	
	23. burned										ed
	24. shirt								ir		
Closed	25. wishes										es
	26. snapped										ed
VCe	27. hiding										ing
	28. racing		soft c								ing

Intermediate Long-Form Spelling Inventory

Basic Syllable Type	Spell Stage / Word	Consonants B	Consonants M	Consonants E	Short Vowel	Digraphs and Blends: digr	Digraphs and Blends: blend	Long Vowel	R-Control	Other/Variant Vowels	Special Consonant	Final Syllable	Prefix	Suffix	Roots	Inflectional Ending
Closed	1. lunch			n		ch										
	2. mesh	m			e	sh										
	3. thistle				i	th					st	le				
	4. wrack				a	ck					wr					
	5. botched	b			o	tch										ed
	6. trampled		m				tr					ple				ed
	7. hungry	h				ng								y		
	8. battle		t									tle				
	9. pennies															es
VCe	10. strove			v			str	o_e								
	11. place						pl	a_e			ce					
	12. while							i_e			wh					
Open	13. tulips							tu								s
	14. flavoring							fla								ing
	15. lightest		t					igh						est		
Vowel team	16. spoiler									oi						er
	17. groom			m						oo						
	18. drawn			n						aw						
R-control	19. deserving								er		s		de		serv	ing
	20. abnormal								or				ab	al	norm	
	21. awareness								are	schwa				ness		
Multisyllable	22. confusion									schwa			con	ion	fus	
	23. invisible										s		in	ible	vis	
	24. disappearance									schwa			dis	ance	appear	
	25. quotient													ent	quot	
	26. judgment										dg			ment	judg	
	27. pleasure													ure	pleas	
	28. naturally								ur					al, ly	nat	

Results of Mrs. W's Spell Inventory
Second Grade 4/22/2016

Most of the class (62 percent or more) has mastered the following:

- Beginning consonant blends (2 and 3)
- Beginning digraphs
- Ending digraphs (except for *ck*)
- Short vowels (*a, e, i, o, u*)
- she (open syllable or sight word)
- *R*-controlled *ar, or*
- *ing* inflectional ending without dropping *e* (*sorting*)

Some of the class (38–61 percent) has mastered the following:

- Inflectional ending ed (*burned*) and ing (*hiding*)
- Open syllable (*pro*)
- Vowel teams (*igh* and *oi*)
- Inflectional ending *es* (*wishes*)

No more than 31 percent of the class has mastered the following:

- *ck* ending
- *dr* beginning blend
- *unk* pattern
- Vowel-consonant-*e* (*o-e, i-e*, etc.)
- Long vowel teams (*ai, ea, oa*)
- Other teams (*oi*)
- Doubling consonant to preserve short vowel (*snapped*)
- Inflectional ending *ed* (*t*, as in *snapped*)
- *R*-control (*ur*)

Results of Mr. K's Spell Inventory
Fifth Grade 4/22/2016

Most of the class (63 percent or above) has mastered the following:

- Beginning consonant blends (2 and 3)
- Beginning digraphs and blends
- Short vowels in single-syllable words (*a, e, i, o, u*)
- VC*e* long vowels (*place* and *rider*)
- Affixes (*con, vis, dis, mis*)

Some of the class (38–63 percent) has mastered the following:

- Short vowels in multisyllabic words (*a, i, e, o*)
- VC*e* (long *i, strive*)
- Inflectional ending *ing* (*serving*)
- C-*le* ending (*trample, battle*)
- Open syllable (*fa, ro, tu*)

No more than 25 percent of the class has mastered the following:

- Vowel teams *oi, igh*
- Change the *y* to *i* and add *es*
- *tch* trigraph
- *sion, tion, sure, ible* endings
- *dge*
- *or* ending /er/ (*favor*)
- Vowel team *ea* (*pleasure*)
- Doubling consonant to preserve short vowel (*snapped*)
- Inflectional ending *est*

Results of Mrs. B's Spell Inventory
Fourth Grade 4/22/2016

Most of the class (75 percent or more) has mastered the following:

- Beginning consonant blends (2 and 3)
- Beginning digraphs and blends
- *tch* ending trigraph
- Short vowels in single-syllable and multisyllabic words (*a, e, i, o, u*)
- VC*e* long vowels
- C-*le* ending (*trample, battle*)
- Open syllable (*fa, ro, tu*)
- Inflectional ending *est, ing*

No more than 38 percent of the class has mastered the following:

- *sion, tion, sure, ible* endings
- *dge*
- *quo*
- Change the *y* to *i* and add *es* (*pennies*)
- Drop the *e*, add *y* (*simply*)
- Affixes with *mis*

First-Grade Nineteen-Step Scope and Sequence for
Spelling, Reading, and Writing

(Adapted from Macmillan/McGraw-Hill's Treasures Reading Program)

Lesson #	Phoneme-Grapheme	Syllable Type	Syllable Rule	Word Bank
1	Short vowel sounds *Grapheme/ phoneme brush-up*	None		A apple /a/ E Ed /e/ I itch /i/ O octopus /o/ U umbrella /u/
2	Short *a* Short *o*	Closed	VC CVC CCVC	at, fat nap, map, snap, sad, dad, tap, slap, flat, flag mop, hop, top, pod, got, hot, log, hog, slop, flop, slot
3	Am, an All	Closed	Welded	ham, jam, slam, fan, can, ran, man, land, sand, hand, stand all, ball, call, fall, hall, mall, tall, wall, stall
4	Short *i* Short *u* Digraphs: *ck, sh*	Closed	*ck* at end of closed syllable, one-syllable word, never at beginning	it, pin, win, hit, sit, slip, flip, spin, pick, slick up, fun, run, cut, nut, rug, flush, slush luck, duck, stuck, stick, ship, fish
5	Short vowels: *a, i, o, u* Digraphs: *ck, sh, ch*	Closed		crab, crop, flag, crib, grab, trap, trip, slip, clock, block, trick, crush, grub, scrap, split, scrub chin, chop, chick, splash
6	Short *e* Digraphs: *ck, ch, sh, th*	Closed		men, ten, pen, bet, let, set, fed, red, sled, leg, beg, get peck, check, fleck, fresh, mesh, shed, bench, then

(continued on next page)

First-Grade Nineteen-Step Scope and Sequence for
Spelling, Reading, and Writing (continued)

(Adapted from Macmillan/McGraw-Hill's Treasures Reading Program)

Lesson #	Phoneme-Grapheme	Syllable Type	Syllable Rule	Word Bank
7	Short vowels: *a, e, i, o, u* *ss, ff, ll*	Closed	Bonus letters (*s, f, l*) in final position of one syllable, closed syllable	back, sack, chop, chin, block, black, clock, stack miss, kiss, grass, brass, loss, boss, stuff, cuff, fluff, stiff, fill, spill, mess, bell, fell, dress, boss, toss, floss
8	*nk* Base word + *s*	Closed	Welded or glued	ink, sink, think, blink, stink, wink, tank, bank, crank, thank, blank, honk, junk, hunk, chunk, stunk thinks, blinks, thanks, winks, honks
9	*ng* (*ing* only)	Closed	Welded or glued Two-syllable short vowels Base word + *ing*	sing, wing, ring, bring, fling, cling, string, thing backing, stacking, gushing, crushing, flushing, calling, falling, thanking, blinking, ringing, thinking, honking, banking
10	Short vowels	Closed	Two-syllable compound words *Chin drop and zap syllables for spelling*	sunset, bobsled, upset, tomcat, hotshot, sunfish, uphill, nutshell, dishpan, shellfish, suntan, bathtub, zigzag, catnip, pigpen, pinball, catfish, puffball, tiptop, cobweb, gunshot, lipstick
11 *	Two-syllable short vowels * Omit this lesson if you think it is too difficult or if more time is needed for previous patterns. Conversely, include this lesson for high-achieving students.	Closed	Two-syllable division CVC-CVC CVC- VC *Chin drop and zap syllables for spelling* *Dividing rule for reading*	napkin, rabbit, picnic, publish, unzip, goblin, invent combat, nutmeg, misfit, public, tennis, muffin finish, panic, limit, cabin, habit, Kevin, topic

(continued on next page)

First-Grade Nineteen-Step Scope and Sequence for Spelling, Reading, and Writing (continued)

(Adapted from Macmillan/McGraw-Hill's Treasures Reading Program)

Lesson #	Phoneme-Grapheme	Syllable Type	Syllable Rule	Word Bank
12	Long *a-e* Long *i-e* *sc, spr, str*	Vowel-consonant-*e* VC*e*		make, take, came, snake, lame, game, gate, late Spike, like, ride, hide, bike, mine string, scrap, strip, spring, strike, scrape, stride, stripe
13	Long *o-e* Long *u-e*	VC*e*		joke, woke, broke, note, vote, hope, poke, slope, rope, stone hose, nose, rose, those, close June, tune, cute, flute, use, fuse, cube, tube, rude
14	Short and long vowels	Closed VC*e*	+ plural *s* *Zap for spelling* *Dividing rule for reading*	pin, pins, cub, cubs, crab, crabs, tube, tubes, clocks, sticks, sunsets, cobwebs, tomcats, goblins snake, snakes, pine, pines, stones, flutes, cubes, plates
15	Long *e: ea* Long *o: oa*	Vowel team	Vowel sound in medial position + plural *s*	seat, beak, bean, bead, teach, cream, scream, screaming, dream, dreaming, team beans, beads, beaks, teams coat, boat, goats, floating, oak, soak, cloak, oats, oatmeal
16	Long *e: ee, y*	Vowel team	Medial position *Y* in final position of multisyllabic word	see, feed, keep, trees, deep, three, green, sheep, queen, greet, street, steep, feeding mushy, tricky, junky, sandy, candy, handy, bumpy, lumpy
17	Long *i: y* Long *e* Long *o*	Open	One-syllable word, vowel not closed by consonant, sound in final position	my, by, fly, why, pry cry, fry, sky, shy, he, she, me, we, be no, go

(continued on next page)

First-Grade Nineteen-Step Scope and Sequence for
Spelling, Reading, and Writing (continued)
(Adapted from Macmillan/McGraw-Hill's Treasures Reading Program)

Lesson #	Phoneme-Grapheme	Syllable Type	Syllable Rule	Word Bank
18	*er*	*R*-controlled Closed Vowel Team	Two-syllable base Closed syllable + *er* Bonus letter VT syllable base word + *er*	her, fern, verb, term, Bert, jerk, perch, stern under, hunter, sticker, sister, thinker, timber, tender, number, finger, thunder filler teacher, sneaker, dreamer
19	*ar, or*	*R*-controlled		or, born, corn, horn, cork, fork, pork, fort, short, shorts, sports, north car, far, star, dark, art, cart, part, start, arm, harm, farm, barn

Spelling List Transformation Examples

In Chapters 3 and 4, we transformed a fourth-grade spelling list in a basal-based classroom and in a balanced literacy classroom. This was done first by focusing the list and then by building it up. Following are list transformations for second and fifth grades.

SECOND GRADE

List in the style of a spelling list from a basal program

card	cardinal*
horn	therefore*
store	sharpen*
part	
harm	
before	
more	
sharp	
scorch	
morning	
chore	
horse	

Focused Super Speller list

card	horn
sharp	scorch
part	morning
harm	horse*
sharpen	

With added words and two-word phrases

far	or	*
star	sort	horse
mark	for	your
hard	born	
arm	short	
farm	porch	
shark	storm	
harm	north	
chart	fork	
marsh	torch	
starting	Ford	
barking	forlorn	
armband	storming	
barnyard	shortstop	
marshmallow	North Star	

List in the style of a spelling list or word sort from a stand-alone program

far	or	more	*
star	sort	store	your
mark	for	chore	
hard	born	tore	
arm	short	shore	
farm	porch	score	
shark	storm	swore	
harm	north		
chart	fork		
marsh	torch		

Focused Super Speller list

far	or	*
star	sort	your
mark	for	
hard	born	
arm	short	
farm	porch	
shark	storm	
harm	north	
chart	fork	
marsh	torch	

With added words

far	or	*
star	sort	horse
mark	for	your
card	born	
hard	horn	
sharp	short	
part	porch	
harm	scorch	
sharpen	storm	
starting	north	
barking	fork	
star chart	torch	
armband	Ford	
barnyard	fork	
marshmallow	storming	
	foghorn	
	forlorn	

FIFTH GRADE

List in the style of a spelling list from a basal program
with focus on consonant sounds *j, ks, sk,* and *s*

scent	joker	justice
muscle	excitement	allergic
scene	except	extremely
explode	fascinate	reminisce
wedge	giraffe	acknowledge
journey	scholar	
scheme	scene	
excuse	lodge	
science	budge	
schedule	schooner	
gigantic		

Focused Super Speller list with focus on consonant sound *j*

journey	giraffe	allergic
justice	gigantic	

With added words

Japan	gem	rigid
jacket	gentle	frigid
jackal	gemstone	tragic
jester	giant	magic
joke	gigantic	digit
jokester	gin	engine
journal	ginger	imagine
journey	gingersnap	apologize
jumble	giraffe	digitize
junior	gym	margin
justice	gyp	angel
prejudice	gypsy	angelic
	gypsum	allergic
	gymnastics	marginal
		digital

List in the style of a spelling list or word sort from a stand-alone program with focus on hard and soft *c* and *g* across vowels

cave	coat	cute	cent	cyst
camp	coast	cups	cell	gym
cast	cost	cue	cease	
gave	gold	gum	gem	
gain	golf	gush	germ	
gasp	goof			

Focused Super Speller list with focus on *g* and *j*

gave	gem	
gasp	germ	
gum	gym	
gush		

With added words

gave	gem	rigid
gasp	germ	frigid
gum	gym	tragic
gush	gentle	magic
gasping	gemstone	digit
joke	giant	engine
Japan	gigantic	imagine
jacket	gin	apologize
jackal	ginger	digitize
jester	gingersnap	margin
	giraffe	angel
	gyp	angelic
	gypsy	allergic
	gypsum	marginal
	gymnastics	digital

Turning Something You *Like* into a *Chore*!

Ladder	Clue
chore	
— — — — —	Something you have to do; work **Change the first two letters to two different letters.**
— — — — —	A place where you can buy things **Change the inside vowel.**
— — — — —	Looking at something for a long time **Change the first letter to two different letters.**
— — — —	Having nothing; to be uncovered **Change the third letter.**
— — — —	To cook a cake in the oven **Change the first letter.**
— — — —	A large body of fresh water **Change the inside vowel.**
like	

SOLUTION
chore
store
stare
bare
bake
lake
like

Turning Your *Feet* into *Hands*!

Ladder	Clue
hands	
— — — — —	**Make the word plural.**
— — — —	You have one on the end of your arm. **Change one letter.**
— — — —	Finely ground rock; a beach is made of this **Change the vowel.**
— — — —	To move something; To put it in the mail **Change a vowel to a consonant.**
— — — —	A plant grows from this. **Change the first consonant.**
— — — —	To give something food **Change the last consonant.**
feet	

SOLUTION
hands
hand
sand
send
seed
feed
feet

Lewis Carroll Doublets

The following are classic Lewis Carroll doublets. When Lewis Carroll presented them to the public, he gave no clues, but he did tell how many steps (or links) were between the first and last word.

Ladder	Clue
tail	
— — — —	Many animals have one **Change one letter.**
— — — —	The opposite of short **Change the vowel.**
— — — —	To say something **Change a vowel to a consonant.**
— — — —	A greenish-blue color **Change the first consonant.**
— — — —	To make someone or something healthy **Change the last consonant.**
head	

SOLUTION
tail
tall
tell
teal
heal
head

Lewis Carroll Doublets (continued)

Ladder	Clue
warm	
— — — —	Opposite of cold **Change the last letter.**
— — — —	A division; a section of a hospital **Change the first letter.**
— — — —	Thick paper cut in a rectangle shape **Change the vowel.**
— — — —	A thick string **Change the third letter.**
cold	

SOLUTION	SOLUTION (easier vocabulary)
warm	warm
ward	harm
card	hard
cord	card
cold	cord
	cold

Lewis Carroll Doublets (continued)

Ladder	Clue
dream	
— — — — —	What you have when you sleep **Make the last letter.**
— — — — —	To feel anxious or afraid **Change the first letter.**
— — — — —	A type of baked food made from flour **Change a vowel.**
— — — — —	One grouping or type of animal **Change the second consonant.**
— — — — —	When blood flows **Change the last consonant.**
— — — — —	A funny sound **Change the first consonant.**
sleep	

SOLUTION
dream
dread
bread
breed
bleed
bleep
sleep

References

Aaron, P., S. Wilcznski, and V. Keetay. 1998. "The Anatomy of Word-Specific Memory." In *Reading and Spelling: Development and Disorders*, ed. C. Hulme and M. Joshi. Mahwah, NJ: Lawrence Erlbaum.

Adams, M. J. 2011. "The Relation Between Alphabetic Basics, Word Recognition, and Reading." In *What Research Has to Say About Reading Instruction*. 4th ed. Ed. S. J. Samuels and A. E. Farstrup. Newark, DE: International Reading Association.

Bear, D. R., M. R. Invernizzi, S. R. Templeton, and F. Johnston. 2012. *Words Their Way: Word Study for Phonics, Vocabulary, and Spelling Instruction*. 5th ed. Boston: Pearson.

Benjamin, A. S., and J. Tullis. 2010. "What Makes Distributed Practice Effective?" *Cognitive Psychology* 61(3): 228–247. doi:10.1016/j.cogpsych.2010.05.004.

Blevins, W. 2001. *Teaching Phonics and Word Study in the Intermediate Grades: A Complete Sourcebook*. 2nd ed. New York: Teaching Resources.

——. 2006. *Phonics from A to Z*. 2nd ed. New York: Teaching Strategies.

Bloom, F., and N. Traub. 2000. *Recipe for Reading*. Revised and expanded. Cambridge, MA: Educators Publishing Service.

Chetty, R., J. N. Friedman, and J. E. Rockoff. 2011. *The Long-Term Impacts of Teachers: Teacher Value-Added and Student Outcomes in Adulthood* (NBER Working Paper No. 17699). Cambridge, MA: National Bureau of Economic Research. Retrieved from www.nber.org/papers/w17699.

Deci, E. 2014. "5 Research-Based Tips for Providing Students with Meaningful Feedback." *Edutopia*, December 29. Retrieved from https://www.edutopia.org/blog/tips-providing-students-meaningful-feedback-marianne-stenger.

Dehaene, S., and L. Cohen. 2011. "The Unique Role of the Visual Word Form Area in Reading." *Trends in Cognitive Science* 15 (6): 254–262.

Dewitz, P., and J. Jones. 2013. "Using Basal Readers: From Dutiful Fidelity to Intelligent Decision-Making." *The Reading Teacher*, 66 (5): 391–400. doi:10.1002/TRTR.01134.

Diamond, L. 2008. *Assessing Reading: Multiple Measures.* 2nd ed. Novato, CA: Arena Press.

Ehri, L. C. 2000. "Learning to Read and Learning to Spell: Two Sides of a Coin." *Topics in Language Disorders* 20(3): 19–36. doi:10.1097/00011363-200020030-00005.

Fletcher, R., and J. Portalupi. 2001. *Writing Workshop: The Essential Guide.* Portsmouth, NH: Heinemann.

Florida Department of Education. 2009. *Phonics Screening Inventory.* Retrieved from http://rti.dadeschools.net/pdfs/phonics_screening_inventory.pdf.

Fry, E. B. 2004. *The Vocabulary Teacher's Book of Lists.* San Francisco: Jossey-Bass.

Gentry, R. 2007. *Assessing Early Literacy with Richard Gentry: Five Phases, One Simple Test.* Portsmouth, NH: Heinemann.

———. 2015. *Current Research on Spelling Instruction.* Retrieved from https://www.zaner-bloser.com/sites/default/files/public/S2731J_Current_Research_on_Spelling_Instruction.pdf.

———. 2016a. *Spelling Connections Teacher Manual.* Columbus, OH: Zaner-Bloser.

———. 2016b. "The Science of Word Sorting." From the *Spelling Connections Teacher Manual.* Columbus, OH: Zaner-Bloser.

Gentry, J. R., and S. Graham. 2010. *Creating Better Readers and Writers: The Importance of Direct, Systematic Spelling and Handwriting Instruction in Improving Academic Performance.* Columbus, OH: Saperstein.

Graham, S. 1998. "Handwriting and Spelling Instruction for Students with Learning Disabilities: A Review." *Learning Disability Quarterly* 22 (2): 78–98.

Graham, S., and K. Harris. 2016. "A Path to Better Writing: Evidence-Based Practices in the Classroom." *The Reading Teacher* 69 (4): 359–365.

Graham, S., K. R. Harris, and C. Loynachan. 1993. "The Basic Spelling Vocabulary List." *Journal of Educational Research* 86 (6): 363–368. Retrieved from http://www.readingrockets.org/article/basic-spelling-vocabulary-list.

Green, S. 2016. *Sylvia Green's Informal Word Analysis.* March 10. Retrieved from http://lincs.ed.gov/readingprofiles/MC_Word_Analysis.htm.

Hattie, J. 2003. "Teachers Make a Difference: What Is the Research Evidence?" Paper presented at the Building Teacher Quality: What Does the Research Tell Us ACER Research Conference, Melbourne, Australia. Retrieved from http://research.acer.edu.au/research_conference_2003/4/.

Hattie, J., and H. Timperley. 2007. *The Power of Feedback: Review of Educational Research.* Retrieved from http://journals.sagepub.com/doi/full/10.3102/003465430298487.

Henderson, E. H. 1990. *Teaching Spelling.* Boston: Houghton-Mifflin.

Invernizzi, M., and L. Hayes. 2004. "Developmental-Spelling Research: A Systematic Imperative." *Reading Research Quarterly* 39 (2): 216–228. doi:10.1598/RRQ.39.2.4.

Levin, I., and D. Aram. 2013. "Promoting Early Literacy via Practicing Invented Spelling: A Comparison of Different Mediation Routines." *Reading Research Quarterly* 48 (3): 221–236.

McCandliss, B., J. Wise, and Y. Yoncheva. 2015. "Hemispheric Specialization for Visual Words Is Shaped by Attention to Sublexical Units During Initial Learning." *Brain and Language* 145–146 (2015): 23–33.

Merriam-Webster. *Merriam-Webster's Pocket Rhyming Dictionary* (Pocket Reference Library). 2001. Springfield, MA: Merriam-Webster.

Moats, L. C. 2005/2006. "How Spelling Supports Reading." *American Educator* (Winter): 12–43. Retrieved from http://www.ldonline.org/article/8845/?theme=print.

Morris, D., L. Blanton, W. W. Glanton, J. Nowacek, and J. Perney. 1995a. "Teaching Low Achieving Spellers at Their Instructional Level." *The Elementary School Journal* 92: 163–177. (In JSTOR.)

——. 1995b. "Spelling Assessment and Achievement in Six Elementary Classrooms." *Elementary School Journal* 96: 145–162. (In JSTOR.)

National Institute of Child Health and Human Development. 2000. *Report of the National Reading Panel. Teaching Children to Read: An Evidence-Based Assessment of the Scientific Research Literature on Reading and Implications for Reading Instruction: Reports of the Subgroups* (NIH Publication No. 00-4754). Washington, DC: U.S. Government Printing Office.

Norton, E. S., I. Kovelman, and L. A. Petitto. 2007. "Are There Separate Neural Systems for Spelling? New Insights into the Role of Rules and Memory in Spelling from Functional Magnetic Resonance Imaging." *Mind Brain Education* 1 (1): 48–59. doi:10.1111/j.1751-228X.2007.00005.x.

Palmer, J. L., and M. Invernizzi. 2015. *No More Phonics and Spelling Worksheets.* Portsmouth, NH: Heinemann.

Perfetti, C. A. 1997. "The Psycholinguistics of Spelling and Reading." In *Learning to Spell: Research, Theory, and Practice Across Languages*, ed. C. A. Perfetti, L. Riegen, and M. Foyl. Mahwah, NJ: Lawrence Erlbaum.

Phenix, J. 2008. *The Spelling Teacher's Book of Lists: Words to Illustrate Spelling Patterns . . . and Tips for Teaching Them.* Markham, ON: Pembroke.

Rapp, B., and K. Lipka. 2011. "The Literate Brain: The Relationship between Spelling and Reading." *Journal of Cognitive Neuroscience* 23 (5): 1180–1197. doi:10.1162/jocn.2010.21507.

Rasinski, T. 2008. *Daily Word Ladders: Grades 1–2: 150+ Reproducible Word Study Lessons That Help Kids Boost Reading, Vocabulary, Spelling, and Phonics Skills.* New York: Scholastic Teaching Resources.

———. 2012. *Daily Word Ladders: 80+ Word Study Activities That Target Key Phonics Skills to Boost Young Learners' Reading, Writing, and Spelling Confidence.* New York: Scholastic Teaching Resources.

Redfield, B. 1986. *Capricorn Rhyming Dictionary.* New York: Perigee Books.

Reed, D. K. 2012. *Why Teach Spelling?* Portsmouth, NH: RMC Research Corporation, Center on Instruction.

Rosenshine, B. 2012. "Principles of Instruction: Research-Based Strategies That All Teachers Should Know." *American Educator* 36 (1): 12–19.

Samuels, S. J., and Y.-C. Wu. 2003. *The Effects of Immediate Feedback on Reading Achievement.* Minneapolis: University of Minnesota. Retrieved from http://www.epsteineducation.com/home/articles/file/research/immediate_feedback.pdf.

Teal, F. Horace. 1892/2016. *English Compound Words and Phrases: A Reference List, with Statement of Principles and Rules* (Classic Reprint). London: Forgotten Books.

Treiman, R. 1993. *Beginning to Spell*. New York: Oxford University Press.

Treiman, R., and D. C. Bourassa. 2000. "The Development of Spelling Skill." *Topics in Language Disorders* 20: 1–18.

Weakland, M. 2014. *Super Core: Turbocharging Your Basal With More Reading, Writing, and Word Work*. Newark, NJ: International Reading Association.

Webb, S. 2007. "The Effects of Repetition on Vocabulary Knowledge." *Applied Linguistics* 28 (1): 46–65. doi:10.1093/applin/aml048.

Willingham, D. T. 2014. *How Did We Learn to Read? Studies Reveal Best Teaching Methods for Kids*. Retrieved from http://www.realcleareducation.com/articles/2014/04/29/how_did_we_learn_to_read_956.html.

———. 2015. *Raising Kids Who Read*. San Francisco: Jossey-Bass.

Wilson, B. 1996. *Dictation Book Steps 1-6*. 3rd ed. Oxford, MA: Wilson Language.

Wilson, B. 1996. *Dictation Book Steps 7-12*. 3rd ed. Oxford, MA: Wilson Language.

Wylie, R. E., and D. D. Durrell. 1970. "Teaching Vowels Through Phonograms." *Elementary English* 47(6): 787–788.

Young, S. 1994. *Scholastic Rhyming Dictionary: Over 15,000 Words*. New York: Scholastic.

Zimmer, C. 2016. "In Science, It's Never 'Just a Theory.'" *New York Times,* December 29. Retrieved from http://www.nytimes.com/2016/04/09/science/in-science-its-never-just-a-theory.

Index

C

D

E

F

G